SUCCESS IN (HIGH) HEELS
30 DAY ~~DIET~~ FEAST TO SUCCESS

Compiled by
Christine Marmoy

Success in (High) Heels - 30 Day ~~Diet~~ Feast to Success

Coaching and Success
c/o Marketing for Coach, Ltd
Second Floor
6th London Street
W2 1HR London

www.coachingandsuccess.com
info@coachingandsuccess.com

ISBN: 978-0-9575561-0-2

Published in UK, Europe, US, Canada and Australia

Book Cover: Karine St-Onge

Inside Layout: Karine St-Onge

Table of Contents

Thank You

I couldn't allow this book to go to press without taking the time to thank a few people. Although I'm well aware that I won't be able to list them all here, I'll do my best!

I would first like to thank my husband Pascal, who has always had faith in me and continually pushes me with his "what if not?" types of questions. I also need to thank—as in big mega-huge kisses—my daughter Camille. She is my first fan and is always so positive and so curious about everything. Please don't ever change; you'll be a great doctor.

A special thanks to Margo DeGange, who encouraged me to pursue my dream with this book just by saying "count me in" on a cold December morning.

A huge thanks to my team, without whom I wouldn't even be in business: to Jane, my loyal and beloved executive assistant, who is my gatekeeper, my sanity savior, my friend, and my rock; to Karine St-Onge, my wonderful graphic designer who always makes sure to represent my work in the best way possible, creating a visual depicting what happens in my head and in my heart; and to Nanette Day, my editor, the newest member of our team, without whose dedication this book wouldn't exist either.

And to all of you dear readers, clients, and Facebook followers, you are helping me grow much more than you think. Thank you!

Introduction

On December 24, my husband turned to me and said "What will you do if you don't get the 30 people you're looking for? Happy Christmas Eve, honey!"

I had just one answer to that question: Why? Quite simply, it had never even crossed my mind that I wouldn't get 30 women to agree to get together and co-create what would become this amazing book. I was confident, I knew the timing was right, and I could no longer ignore the cry from my heart.

Two years ago, I had conjured up the format for the perfect anthology book—one that would be able to serve as many women as possible, throughout the world. So what happened to that idea? It went into hibernation, like so many others before it, and ended up in a forgotten, dusty corner of my mind…until today.

This book is a true testimony to what one woman can achieve when she understands that being a woman is her greatest asset in life and in business. Since the 1990s, we have been brainwashed into thinking that, to be successful in business, we had to behave like our role models at the time—meaning our male counterparts. However, we came to realize that this strategy was only a springboard to failure for most of us.

We had been taught to model ourselves on what we were expected to become, yet in some instances, that might not have been the best lesson for us. We are so different from men, and that in itself is good. In fact, it's great because, by realizing this, it means we can fully step forward toward success in a feminine way.

Men run their businesses pretty much like playing a game. They go in with just one goal in mind: to win. Women, on the other hand, will get involved in a venture if it allows them to belong to a group and collaborate. Winning is only a consequence of the game; the goal here is to be together.

We don't relate to rules in the same way. For us, rules are guidelines that come under the "information" banner, whereas for men, rules are carved in stone and must be adhered to. We cut corners; they follow a straight path. We communicate; they don't, really. We collaborate; they go it alone whenever they get the chance.

So how do you expect to win the game if you take on a role that is not your own? The answer is very straightforward: You can't.

We, as women, are natural leaders and collaborators; this is where our strength lies, and we can't ignore it in order to win the game. It is the very asset that will enable us to win the game of succeeding in business.

I very often say that success is built with others, because that is the truth. This book would never have seen the light of day if it had not been for the great collaboration that took place before it ended up in your hands.

Our world is changing. Although I've never believed in the catastrophic scenario of the end of our world, I have always had the feeling that some kind of shift was really happening. I honestly believe that we can shape a better world—that we have the power, the willingness, and the skill to step in and give our society as we know it a different direction and in a much broader way—in order to have a much bigger impact on the decisions that have to be made to ensure that our economy as well as our social and educational system thrives in every situation.

We are no better than men in any shape or form; we are simply different. This difference is what will forge a real change in the way the world develops.

We are natural leaders, even if you don't realize it. You are a leader in your home, in your life, and in your business. Now you might not feel confident enough to fully embrace this role, but believe me: You are.

Being a leader also means understanding that, to lead, you need a crowd to be led. By crowd, I mean collaborators, colleagues, and staff. You'll need to surround yourself with all these different disciplines—maybe not all at the same time, but at some point you'll need to work with a few people—so be open and receptive to the challenges the universe brings your way and make sure you gather the right team around you. That team will become the backbone of your business.

In my experience, I have come across a few ways to make someone shine. You can push people down and, through cause and effect, you are the one who will automatically shine through. But don't forget about karma: What goes around, comes around. By acting in such a way, you could destroy your self-confidence for a long time to come. Alternatively, you can identify your weaknesses and then start out on the never-ending quest for perfection. I've been there and done that. Let me tell you that you'll never get to the point where you are truly satisfied because nobody's perfect and you'll end up getting burned out. Or—and this is the best way I know of—you make a list of what you are good at and put all your efforts into doing things that are using these very talents. This approach is faster and easier, and it will boost your self-esteem while filling up your bank account.

Collaboration is the main toolset for women because it is a true inherent talent. Many women dismiss collaboration as being too "girly," arguing that modern society can perceive it as a weakness, thereby giving rise to an "unreliable and unstable" side of our persona, as if we needed to be more manly to guarantee our success.

Women—and I'm sure you'll recognize yourself in this—love gathering around a cause. Find that cause, that "why" that will serve everybody in the process—you, your collaborators, and, to a certain extent, the world—and fully step into the leader's role: Innovate and discover what you could unearth that would make your collaborators say "I'm in" while having a bigger agenda.

The following pages are testimony to the fact that anything can be done when you put your mind to it as long as it is aligned with who you are deep down in your soul.

I'm a "socialholic," and yes, I'm proud to be one. However, I don't like spending too much time chatting aimlessly at networking events. Such events can be great, but somehow I always feel like they are not so "action oriented." For me, networking events have a social dimension. I like meeting new people and I like making new friends, then once I get that idea—that "thing" that I really have to do—I know who to call on. That is how I use my collaborative networking, as I like to call it. I make friends because I'm social and love meeting new people; then I collaborate.

Now, don't imagine that you have to be out and about 3 days a week getting involved in all sorts of networking events because that is a false belief. I gathered together 30 amazing women to co-create this book while sitting at my desk in Spain. And from here, I managed to have the book represented in Germany, the United Kingdom, the United States, Canada, Australia, the Bahamas, and Spain. Not bad, eh? And I didn't even have to travel.

Although I love to travel and I adore meeting new people and networking, the point I want to make to you is that you don't have to do it. Don't invent limitations where there are none. Where there is a will, there is a way—this saying holds true about everything.

What would I like this book to give you?

You know, I've been thinking of many different issues, but I took a day or two to really reflect on what I wanted these few pages to do for you.

My wish is for this book to change your life. You might balk and claim that this is a far-fetched dream, yet I am sure that we can all recall a book that triggered something in our mind to the point where it subsequently influenced the direction of our life. That is exactly what I hope this book will do for you. I want it to help you take that first step toward change—change in your life as much as in your business.

That is why this book is not strictly limited to business concepts. I'm a firm believer that, to be truly successful in our business, we need to take care of ourselves first, which includes our family, our social circle, our health, and our well-being in general.

How can you use this book to fully benefit from it?

As all of you, dear beautiful readers, come from different walks of life, different points in your life and in your business, there is no specific order in which you should read the following pages. You can pick and choose the chapter(s) that most resonate with you and do the same with all the other ones, or you can read them from start to finish. It's entirely up to you.

Each chapter, from 1 to 30, is a lesson. Each lesson will teach you a very important point in business and/or in life to help you reach that place you call success. As no change really happens without implementation, each lesson contains an exercise to help you start the meaningful change that you are seeking.

I personally hand-picked all the women who share their expertise in this book, and I wanted you to know how I came to choose them. I set a few specific criteria to follow: Each one had to have a vision for the world, each had to be working with women, each had to walk the talk and be honest, each had to be professional so we could keep to the deadlines set, each had to be authentic, and all of them had to be fun to work with. Having fun is very important for me, and I wanted to make sure I had a fantastic time with all of the co-creators during this entire project.

And guess what? They were all just amazing! They all exceeded my expectations and, when I read their chapters over a weekend, I became very emotional. As the tears were running down my cheeks, I made the wish that you, my dear special readers, would be touched in just the same way as I was.

Embark on this journey with us, and your life will never be the same again.

~Christine

Sue Donnelly

"Sue has a passion for fashion and style and is one of the most qualified consultants working in the image industry."

She is quirky, fun, empathetic, daring, and open to new ideas and the concept of change. She has a holistic approach that often challenges the norm, making her very innovative and individualistic in the way she works with people. She makes fashion, image, and personal branding exciting, fun, and inspirational. Her ability to make authentic style achievable in a way that is totally relevant, meaningful, and practical for each individual is one of her strengths. She is sensitive and caring, with a creative style of her own that sets her apart from the crowd.

www.suedonnelly.com

 https://www.facebook.com/Suejdonnelly

. . . .

I invited Sue to participate in this project because I truly believe that she has a different approach to style, fashion, and clothes. For her, we all have the right to be and feel fabulous, using clothes as the catalyst. Sue is a breath of fresh air. She is incredibly funny and easy to work with. She is fast, she is professional, and she has the talent of being able to teach women how to use their wardrobe to be magnificent in their business.

Whether you are a fashion addict or not, your appearance has a direct impact on your self-confidence and on the value you portray to your clients. I couldn't omit this subject in a book that speaks the truth about success.

Thank you, Sue, for being part of this adventure.

{ LESSON 1 }

HOW TO DRESS FOR AUTHENTIC SUCCESS
by Sue Donnelly

As female entrepreneurs, we are—by our very nature—trendsetters. Without a "boss" to answer to, we have the freedom and flexibility to change the world, business models, and timetables in order to seek out and serve our perfect clients. It's not fair, but it is true that we judge people according to their appearance. Your clothing acts as a very important aspect of your potential business success. Whether you like it or not, your image acts as visual shorthand, speedily expressing who you are, what you stand for, your talents and your abilities—all in a matter of seconds! Nobody advocates style over substance, but attaining congruency and consistency between how you look and other key factors is critical if you are to be authentic in every aspect of your business.

To be successful in your image, you need to think about 3 different factors:

1. Does it truly convey who you are, what you believe in, your standards, your values, your ethics, and what you want to say to the world about yourself? Does what you sell also fit these criteria?

2. Is it appropriate for the occasion, your objectives, your intentions, and your audience's expectations? Is what you're selling appropriate to the level of clients you are servicing/ seeking?

3. Does what you wear fit you properly and flatter your physicality? Is your business a good "fit" for you and what you stand for?

I call these elements Style for your Soul (1), Spirit (2) and Silhouette (3). All three need to be in place if you are to be comfortable and authentic in what you are wearing. The more often you look and feel great, the more confident you become and, as a result, attracting strong and profitable client relationships becomes easier. Thinking about the clients you want to attract is a great starting point. If they are high-earning executives, your choice of clothing might be very different to that of a spiritual, holistic, or more creative marketplace.

We are all unique. Copying a style because it suits someone else is nigh on impossible. The following exercise will help you understand your preferences about dress and how your shopping habits and image management might differ from those around you.

A. Do you covet the latest trends and constantly change your look?

B. Do you prefer quality tailoring that allows easy coordination of your clothes?

C. Do you love pretty, feminine clothes and prefer skirts to trousers?

D. Are you a wash'n'go type of person who opts for a more natural, relaxed look?

E. Do you create a statement by using the unusual, such as a great piece of jewelry, a funky hairstyle, or clothes in strong color combinations?

If you are most like answer a, then you are a **creative/innovative** dresser. You love rummaging through charity shops and vintage stores to find eclectic items that you can throw together. Chain stores hold no appeal as they are too "mass market." You crave individuality and artistry.

If you resonated with answer b, you are a **classic/elegant** dresser. You love garments that stand the test of time and always look smart due to their tailoring. You prefer a coordinated approach to dressing, so colors are rarely mixed. Fashion trends do not interest you, but quality does.

If you selected c as your answer, you love the feminine; masculine attire does not interest you. You are a **romantic/feminine** dresser. Pretty colors, florals, patterns, and floating fabrics are the essence of your wardrobe. Your clothes might not be too structured, but you pay attention to the detail.

If you picked d as the answer most like you, then you are a **natural/ sporty** dresser. You might have leanings toward sporty clothes, such as trainers and T-shirts, rather than high heels and blouses or just prefer natural fabrics with little or no structure. Relaxed and comfortable are your key words. You wear minimal jewelry and little or no makeup, with hair tied back or flowing loose around your face.

The answer e reflects a **dramatic/alluring** dresser. You create attention by using unique and individual accessories or a bold use of color. You might be high maintenance and you might also have lots of clothes that have been worn once (someone might have seen it before!). Clothes make a statement about you and, even if you're not aware of it, you will be noticed.

Creative/innovative dressers can choose belts, scarves that don't coordinate, vintage pieces, unusual brooches or corsages, crocheted shrugs, feather boas, or anything that looks slightly eccentric to show off their look to the maximum. Mixing textures such as wool and chiffon can also work, as long as doing so doesn't add unwanted bulk. You can be seen as quite "artsy," so be aware of audience/industry expectations if a more sedate approach is required.

Classic/elegant dressers can mix and match existing garments with any new purchases. Try to vary your look by bringing in some color. Simplicity and understatement are key to your look, so beware of wearing too many pieces of jewelry at once. Although you might prefer the real thing, try good quality costume jewelry if you want to add some variety. To modernize, wear flesh-colored fishnet tights or softly patterned dark opaque tights. Handbags and shoes should no longer match exactly, so keep the colors the same but change fabric types. Make sure that your garments are classic, but not dated, if you want to be perceived as business savvy.

Romantic/feminine dressers can look great in garments that have some appliqué, beading, or diamante. Soft layers, floating fabrics, and frills in chiffon or lace are your style. Select luxurious fabrics, such as cashmere, satin, and silk, for both outerwear and underwear. Soft, pretty cardigans or jackets in a softer, more pliable fabric might look better than a suit jacket. Floral prints and abstracts can work well, but keep the occasion and your intention in mind. Woven or decorative handbags look better than stiff leather.

Natural/sporty dressers look best in natural fabrics and neutral colors. For you, linen, wool, suede, and leather in loose-fitting styles will make the best jackets. Choose comfortable shoes, but try to make them modern; for example, ballet pumps can look great with jeans or a skirt. Jersey dresses and jackets are easy to wear and can look natural and stylish at the same time. Remember, though, that being relaxed does not mean not making an effort. In the business world, this can be seen as lazy. A pair of pearl earrings and some mascara and lip gloss are your essentials.

Dramatic/alluring dressers need to look for key pieces that add impact. Wear unusual buckles on your belt, eye-catching spectacles, a huge ring, a unique bag, or killer shoes. Alternatively, add a streak of color to your hair, wear colored mascara, and paint your lips in bright or dark red or pink. Bold colors suit your style and your attitude. Just be aware that you can look "untouchable" in some circumstances, and you might need to soften your approach.

Once you have uncovered your style personality, you'll need to look at how it aligns with your business. If you are romantic by nature, but need to appear authoritative, wear a suit by all means, but soften it with a feminine blouse. Alternatively, ask yourself is this the type of business you want to be doing? Wearing a uniform that does not belong to you is called "acting."

Finally, you should follow some rules of thumb whatever your type:

- Fit is everything, whatever the cost; if it doesn't fit, it looks cheap.

- Before you buy something, look at yourself from all angles, sit down, and move your arms. You need to be comfortable, with no horizontal drag lines along the shoulder, across the thigh, or under the arms.

- High contrast, stiffer fabrics and/or angular lines provide instant authority. To soften the approach, blend colors and use texture or malleable fabrics, such as jersey. Losing the jacket and swapping a suit for a dress will also work.

Think of what you want to get out of your meeting. Who will be there? What do they expect from you? What is your objective? You need to dress with these ideas in mind. If a huge change of image is involved, ask yourself: "Is this what I really want?" Your clothes speak volumes to your audience, but they will also communicate with you too, if you give them the chance.

Image breakers include overpowering fragrance, jangling jewelry, bad breath, smoking, too much makeup, tardiness, and bad manners—but I am going to guess that you know that already.

Successful brands are consistent in their approach so we know what to expect from them. You need to be the same. Your image is only one component of a successful business. Behavior and communication are equally as important and, along with appearance, form the basis of your reputation. Be aware of what you want to be remembered for. We all have an image, whether or not we take the time to cultivate it.

Bunny Star

Bunny Star is the founder, owner, and director of Hoop Empire. She is a multimedia artist who has been working as lead hula hoop performer, manufacturer, and teacher to both adults and children for the past seven years, which were preceded by an additional 13 years of hoop play. Bunny holds a Bachelor of Arts in writing and history. She is also an avid student of Western Sun Sign Astrology and the 13 Moon Mayan Dreamspell.

http://www.hoopempire.com

http://bunnyhoopstar.wordpress.com

https://www.facebook.com/HoopEmpire

https://www.facebook.com/bunnyhoopstar

My encounter with Bunny Star proves the benefits of a well-managed Facebook account. I met her through one of my pages. I had talked about this project and the anthology, and she went all out about it, saying, "I'm interested in participating."

The next thing I knew, I had fallen in love with an authentic power. She is one of a kind and is worth being known. She built her first business based on passion and is currently doing it again. You'll learn a lot from Bunny, I can promise you that much.

Thank you, Bunny. I hope I'll be able to hug you very soon. This book wouldn't have been the same without you.

{ LESSON 2 }

PASSION, POWER, PURPOSE: TRANSFORMING YOUR HOBBY INTO A WAY OF LIFE

by Bunny Star

. . . .

Passion, power, and purpose—as a golden triangle mantra—give me the tools to live the life I want to live. Passion is a true measure of desire, an indicator of just how much we want what we are after and how willing we are to pursue, enjoy, and sustain it. Power suggests an ability to radiate energy that creates extraordinary transformation and abundant life, just like the Sun. Purpose is a sense of self-direction informed by a greater source than the mind and that points toward giving back to life itself in gratitude. What do we have to offer this world as individuals and communities that honor the life we live?

I have come to realize that, once I identify my passion and give it the attention it needs and deserves, I am more capable of stepping into my power and fulfilling my purpose on this planet. Part of that purpose is to invite you to join me on this journey and tap into your own golden treasures as a way in which to enrich your life through personal growth and creative transformation.

You will need more than one hobby for this lesson in creative transformation and a willingness to take a risk. What does it take to live your heart's true desire as a job, career, or way of life? It takes time, intention, focus, devotion, frustration, elation, alienation, confusion, clarity, commitment, community, practice, resources, a mountain to climb whose peak is often out of sight, and a strong steady focus on each small step. It is often unruly and highly disorganized because it is only you, playing all the roles in order to live the dream of having

14

the freedom to create what you want, when you want. Where do you start and how do you stop (as there is not much reason to stop—you love it) as there is always something to do? When you transform your hobby into a job or career, what replaces your playtime? Are you willing to hand over what you love to "The Man"—that is, you? Are you prepared and equipped to be your own boss? How does it feel to know that every single cent that you earn (or don't) is your complete responsibility? What if you become sick or are unable to work? These are all essential questions to consider when making a dive into the unknown realm of developing a creative and self-directed career. You can go as fast or as slow as you like; this journey is yours. What this lesson points to is the possibility for rich personal and professional fulfillment when we embrace our passion and make it an essential part of everyday life through our jobs, careers, or relaxation time. In this way we can explore the breadth of the gifts and talents that we were born with and that beckon our attention throughout life as a subtle and intuitive calling.

I am a hoop dancer based in Sydney, Australia, and often travel the world on hoop missions that have my name on them. For the past seven years, I have performed, taught, and made hula hoops as a full-time job. I also write, develop, and present programs and projects that cultivate aspects of the practice, such as hoop dance technique, performance skill training, and a global children's program that is currently in development. I hold a degree in creative writing and history and I love to tell a good story.

It all started on a dance floor 20 years ago in Melbourne. I was dancing in a club when the show began: A stunning circus star appeared with countless silver hoops spinning all over her body. I was struck with such awe and amazement that what she was doing was even possible and that she made it look so easy. There could not have been a more perfect point for a sign to fall from the sky, screaming prepare yourself for the most magical adventure of your life! I could not have dreamt in that moment that this experience would ignite what was to follow—a hoop disco inferno comes close to describing it.

I moved to Sydney a few years later and bumped into that very circus star who had hit the dance floor with my destiny. We played with hoops; she showed me tricks and I had a lot of fun, but it was difficult and, as a slow learner, it took me a long time. Circus style hula hooping requires a lot of training in strict Russian- and Chinese-inspired styles that command discipline, strength, alignment, and a "more is more" approach. The number of hoops you can spin is important. Your goal is the stage. I have to admit I wasn't so drawn to this approach as much as I tried. Hooping was play for me, so the intense training and hard work aspect seemed not to fit with what I wanted from it, which was enjoyment. In addition, there was no way I was going to be a performer—I was too shy!

A few more years passed and I started to notice a growing online community of hoop dancers, based primarily in the United States. It was 2006 and the Burning Man festival was on the schedule, so off to the hoop dance mecca I did go to find my tribe. The first thing I discovered was that hoop dancers are the rebels of the circus. The hoop dance style breaks many circus hula movement rules that I would not be showing off in China or Russia. For hoop dancers, the utmost priority is feeling good while rocking out with a single hoop, maybe two. Innovating new tricks and moves, studying technique and philosophy, sharing, exploring, and playing for play's sake are also common features. Hoop dancers are not necessarily in it for the performance, but are definitely in it for the fun, sparkle, and community. They know that a big heavy hoop can be used as a fitness or dance tool for all shapes, sizes, and fitness levels and can get almost anyone hooping who wants to but can't. They also know that hooping is therapeutic for children of all ages and that to dance you need to move your body and soul. The rules of the circus went flying out the window as I spun on turbo with full commitment. Be it on stage or on the dance floor, I had found the vehicle through which to express my love of the hoop: dance.

To spin on stage was to say no to feeling shy or unsure of myself and yes to stepping up to my full potential. I had some hoop skills by then as well as a wild wardrobe, so as I started my performance career as a 33-year-old woman, I felt fairly confident that I could pull it off… and if I didn't, valuable lessons would come from taking a risk and allowing my career path and daily job to be directed by a passion that lived in my heart: to play, dance, and create. A hoop troupe was born so that we could perform. We toyed with two names: The Barbarellas and The Hoopaholics. The latter won and, with a serious training schedule, we were well on the way to being Australia's one and only hoop dance troupe. Today we are known as Platinum (transformation is key to the process of creative exploration). One show led to another, with our hoopla gracing stages from local community festivals to exclusive corporate events, nightclubs, private parties for adults and kids, public art exhibitions…the list is long. What was even more amazing to watch was the two other arms of this highly lucrative business grow organically from our fun for everyone's communal approach. By inviting one and all to give it a whirl through interactive shows, community hoop jams, and local classes, "non-hoopers" came to expect their own rite of passage with the hoop—and they got it, although they needed bigger hoops than those being sold in toy stores. From this demand we began hand crafting and selling hoops that were suitable for all to use. Creating an online presence was essential to spreading our hoop love far and wide. Hoop Empire, the name of my growing business, now offers classes all over Sydney, online learning programs, an instructional DVD, stunning hoops including light hoops, and retreats both within and outside of Australia. It is partnered with several other hoop businesses nationally and worldwide. The hoop tricked me into signing up for the hardest work I have ever encountered in exchange for endless play.

My entire life has been transformed by this conscious decision to set my own rules and spend the majority of my waking life doing what I love. The beliefs that held me back no longer exist, and the shyness is almost unnoticeable. The powerful magic of the hula hoop has guided me through thick and thin. It has kept me connected with my child within, a part of me which holds my true essence. After 20 years on the hoop disco dance floor, I am ready to spin my cocoon and transform yet again into whatever appears before my eyes. The urge to write and share insights on living a dreamy hoop-filled life pops onto the page as just one way of transforming passions and dreams into reality. The beauty of taking life into your own hands and making the big decisions is that the only limit is imagination and the ability to decipher the puzzle of putting the dream pieces together so that the visual reality emerges.

By actively jumping on board a journey of self-inquiry and applying it to your daily life, the possibility of expressing the full creative potential while giving back to the world becomes very real. Here is a guide on how to get started in three easy steps:

1. JOURNAL

Find a beautiful book to write in that inspires you. Write a list of all the things you enjoy doing and identify which of those you would consider to be your passions, with numbers that indicate order of importance. Highlight the one(s) that you can see yourself investing more time and energy into purely because you feel drawn to them in perhaps an unexplainable but powerful way.

2. FIND THE COMMON THREAD

Are there any shared underlying themes with your numerous hobbies and passions, such as healing, creativity, art, food preparation, nutrition, nature, exercise, skill development, learning, childcare, animals, or anything else? If so, consider how these hobbies could possibly connect with, or distract from, one another? You want to be as focused and expansive as possible.

3. CONNECT WITH COMMUNITY

Find the experts and communities, both on- and offline, who are already living a similar dream to connect, research, be inspired, and get started. Follow the steps that others have taken before you. The more support you have and material you have to draw from, the easier it will be to activate your passion or hobby into an important aspect of your life, be it job, career, or part-time love. Work toward your goal one step at a time.

The most challenging aspect of turning dreams into reality is believing that you can succeed and being prepared to commit to your visions. Actually doing it is about working out how the dream machine works by becoming an imagineer (and a director, producer, performer, critic, bookkeeper, and ticket seller) who knows how to design and construct the stage so that everything synergizes to create the play that is your life. It won't happen automatically or immediately, but if you are determined and focused, it will happen. We live in a time of such momentous inspiration, information, innovation, and entrepreneurial opportunity that, if there is a little voice calling you to step up to a different stage in life, I am here to say GO FOR IT! It is possible, powerful, and filled with passion and purpose. This is living life with a full cup ready to toast—a salute to all that is you.

Kelly Falardeau

Kelly Falardeau has been a burn survivor since she was two years old who has constantly struggled with her self-esteem and inner beauty. She found a way to go from near-death to success; from the ugly scar-faced girl to the Top 10 Most Influential Speakers, Fierce Woman of the Year, two-time best-selling author, and recipient of the Queen Elizabeth II Diamond Jubilee Medal. You have to ask yourself: How? How did a burn survivor who constantly struggled with rejection, staring, and teasing burst through all the negativity in her life to succeed?

www.KellyFalardeau.com

KellyFalardeau – Speaker

@KellyFalardeau

. . . .

Top Ten Most Influential Speakers
Best-selling Author
Recipient of the Queen Elizabeth Diamond Jubilee Medal
Fierce Woman of the Year

I also discovered Kelly through Facebook, thanks to our common friend, Aime Hutton (also featured in this book). I was instantly moved by her story, but I was especially inspired by her creativity. The way she was using her story was, to my eyes and to my heart, quite exceptional. When this project came to the forefront, I was hoping she'd say yes—and obviously she did. She was about to leave for Kenya; nevertheless, she jumped on board will a full "I'm in!"

Thank you, Kelly. Nobody could have covered the topic of inspiration better than you.

{ LESSON 3 }

TAKING THE "T" OUT OF CAN'T

by Kelly Falardeau

One of the biggest questions I get is "how do you do that?" How do you walk out the door even with scars on your face? How did you start your balloon store? How did you create a mobile scrapbook store? How did you write your book? How did you turn two books into best sellers? How did you become a speaker? How did you become one of the Top 10 Most Influential Speakers? How did you become the Fierce Woman of the Year? How did you walk the runway and win the People's Choice Award? How do you get so much media coverage for your story?

Yes, a gazillion questions about how I lived my life. How did I face all the adversity? How did I get over the staring and teasing? How did I handle the bullying and name-calling? How do you do so much stuff? How did you become a recipient of the Queen Elizabeth Diamond Jubilee Medal?

Yes, a gazillion more questions. I won't be able to answer all the questions in this chapter, but I will be able to help you with the "how." How did I learn how to take the "T" out of can't. How did I do so much stuff? Saying "can't" wasn't an option in my family. If I wanted something, I had to find a way to get it or forget about it.

One thing I learned is that my parents and family never let me quit. My scars were never an issue. I got burnt when I was two years old. So what?! Why does that make me any different than anyone else? My parents didn't think I was different, nor should I have been treated any differently. I was just Kelly, nothing more, nothing less. I had a tragic accident when I was two and was burned on over 75% of my body, resulting in countless surgeries until I was 21 years old. I had to endure staring, teasing, and rejection my whole life. So what?! Suck it up and quit feeling sorry for yourself. That was what my parents said. I didn't think I should be treated any differently just because I had scars. I just wanted to blend in and be like everybody else.

My grandma said, "Kelly, you have to stick up for yourself no matter what." That's what I did. I didn't hesitate to tell someone they were wrong or to quit bugging me. If they were snotty with me about my scars, I was snotty back and walked away. I didn't let them get me down.

No matter what I wanted to do, my parents allowed me to do (within reason of course). When I asked if I should try out for the cheerleading squad, my mom's response was, "Well, why not?" She never said to me, "Kel, you're going to get teased because everyone is going to be staring at you." I was never allowed to quit just because I had scars.

I just thought I was a normal kid, but with scars. No, I didn't like my scars and many, many times I wished I didn't have them. I used to pray at night when I was a teenager for God to take my scars away and make me pretty like all the other girls. I just wanted to fit in. I had lots of friends, but I knew the bullies were calling me the ugly scar-faced girl. Yet even amongst all the staring, teasing, and rejection I didn't let it stop me from getting what I wanted.

I never had boyfriends in school, but when I was 19 I met my husband (who is now my ex-husband) and we were together for 24 years. We had four beautiful children, including our daughter, a stillborn angel baby, and our twin sons. Having children was something I never thought I could do. I didn't think burnt people had babies. When I found out that, in fact, other burn survivors had kids, I realized that I could too, and we started planning a family. I was concerned whether my scars would stretch enough in order for me to have babies, but I was wrong. Burn survivors do have babies, and the skin can stretch enough.

Throughout my life I was always one of those people who got bored very easily. I used to admire how my grandma could work at one job her whole life. I could never last at the same job for more than 2.5 years and I used to wonder why. Some people might say that it's

ADD, but I prefer to think it's just because I get bored easily and like to do whatever inspires me at the time. I like to do many different things—and I'm not the crazy one!

When I get it in my head that I want to write a book about self-esteem, I just do it. When I get my "aha" moments, I act on them. Those "aha" moments are bursts of energy that you need to make things happen. I know when I don't act on them, I lose them, and I don't like losing that energy. Those "aha" moments inspire me and get me through my life.

For example, at one time my passion was scrapbooking. All I wanted to do was scrapbook. I knew I wanted to make it my business, but I couldn't figure out how. I knew I didn't want a typical brick-and-mortar scrapbook store because I had twin baby boys and didn't want to be tied to the high overhead costs and time commitments. So I asked my ex-husband what he thought of me creating a "mobile" scrapbook store. His response was, "That's brilliant, when are you starting?" I thought it was a crazy idea, but he didn't think so.

Six months later, I had a business plan, financing, a 14-cubic-foot van converted into a store (by my ex-husband), a website, marketing, and bookings in place waiting for me to come. He told me to go for it, so I did. I didn't let fear stop me; I moved forward. I just knew in my heart and soul it was the right thing to do. I had a vision for it, a passion, and the drive to make it happen. Nothing was going to stop me. Three years later I sold it as a successful business to another lady who wanted to make it her passion, and I became a speaker and author.

WHAT IS THE LESSON?

How do you take the "T" out of can't? Quite simply. Quit saying to yourself, "I can't do that." If there is something you really want to do, don't say "I can't do that," because when you do, your mind will agree with you and say "yes, you're right, you can't do it." It's only natural that you won't be able to achieve your goal because you've already convinced yourself that you can't do it before you even tried. If you really want to do it, you need to take the "T" out of can't and say to yourself, "How can I do that?" That is the correct question to ask. When you ask yourself "How can I do that?" you open up your mind to the **possibility** of doing it, and your mind will come up with the solution on **how** to do it. You might not get the answer instantly, but it will come.

When you ask yourself a question, your conscious mind generally wants to find an answer. If you just give yourself a statement that says "I can't do that," you're right, you can't and your mind won't even try to find a way to do it. Your mind will just agree with you. It is as simple as that. So, to take the "T" out of can't, just ask yourself: "How can I do ___?" (and fill in the blank).

For example, when I decided I wanted to write a book with 1000 tips for teens, I could have had two different thoughts. I could have thought "I can't write a book of 1000 tips for teens—that would be impossible, I don't know 1000 tips" or "How can I write a book of 1000 tips for teens?" Obviously, I thought the latter question because the book is written and now a #1 best seller.

When I asked myself how, the answer came quickly: How about asking 100 people to write 10 tips each and then you'll get your 1000 tips written for you? So that's what I did. I started asking people for their tips and *voilà* we had a book written. So don't say to yourself "I can't do that"; instead ask "How can I do that?" and the answer will come to you eventually.

Dr. Anna Garrett

Dr. Anna Garrett is Chief Mojo Officer at **www.drannagarrett.com.** She is a clinical pharmacist and certified intrinsic coach. Whether navigating menopause or the challenges of entrepreneurship, Dr. Anna's goal in business is to help women feel better—it's that simple!

In 2011, she launched Dr. Anna Garrett (**www.drannagarrett.com**). She now coaches women on how to maximize their mojo through menopause and create a solid foundation of wellness in midlife. Dr. Anna offers a variety of hormone balancing and wellness coaching services.

Download Dr. Anna's Weekly Mojo Manager at
http://www.drannagarrett.com/free-resources/

. . . .

Having had some health issues, I knew first hand that nobody could really succeed without a great dose of well-being. Too often I hear women telling me that they can't take it anymore—that they are at the end of what they can possibly endure and they have no more energy left for anything, even less their business. Well, it doesn't have to be this way, and that is a promise. It was very important for me to find the right woman to address this issue in a way that would entice you to take "you" very seriously.

Thank you, Anna, for being so quick to accept my invitation. Your chapter represents exactly what I wanted to see in this book, and it is a true gift to our readers.

{ LESSON 4 }

YOUR BUSINESS DEPENDS ON YOUR HEALTH: THE 8 P'S OF CREATING A SOLID WELLNESS FOUNDATION

by Anna D. Garrett, PharmD, BCPS, CIC®, CVS-FR

. . . .

When it comes to maintaining good health, being a self-employed entrepreneur is great—if you are health conscious to begin with. However, if creating rockin' health mojo is not high on your priority list, the stresses of running a business (especially if you are a solopreneur) increase the likelihood of making choices that don't support your mind, body, or spirit. This creates a vicious cycle. Your lack of time and attention to yourself leads to fatigue and the "I don't feel like it" syndrome. Before you know it, your body—with its toxic load of stress, bad food, and flabby muscles—has becomes a "bad neighborhood" for your business.

Your body is a complex network of systems. When one part of the system goes off track, it all goes off track. Ignoring a crack in a piece of your foundation won't make things better and could ultimately lead to a roaring case of burnout or a chronic illness.

No thanks to that.

So what's a busy, up-and-coming business owner to do?

1. PRIORITIZE: PUT YOURSELF ON YOUR TO-DO LIST

In order to create balance and move toward a healthier lifestyle as an entrepreneur, your health should be one of your top 3 priorities. If not, both you and your business could potentially suffer the consequences of living in a bad neighborhood. **Don't take your health for granted.**

Give yourself (and your business) the gift of a conscious commitment to creating the healthiest you possible!

2. PLAN: CREATE SYSTEMS AND HABITS TO SUPPORT YOU

The key to implementing healthy strategies is balance; in order to have balance, you need routine. Creating a routine requires planning. Entrepreneurs often struggle with creating and maintaining structure in their daily lives because they're frequently pulled in many directions. We all know that infants and young children thrive on routine and structure. **Why not apply this principle to ourselves?**

Here are several great places to start:

- Get up and go to bed at the same time every day (even weekends). Aim for 7-8 hours of sleep. This allows your body to repair itself and keeps weight gain away!

- Eat on a regular schedule. Your body was not designed to eat at random times during the day. Going too long without a meal or snack causes it to think it's going into starvation mode (causing it to release cortisol). Eating at scheduled times goes a long way toward keeping your cortisol levels in check and preventing blood sugar swings. Set a timer if you need to remind yourself to do this.

- Schedule exercise time just as you would any meeting. Plan what you are going to do and for how long. Vary your workouts so your body doesn't get used to one routine. Hire a personal trainer to keep you accountable or, if the cost is prohibitive, hire one for a few sessions to help you design a workout you can do at home.

- Take frequent breaks from work. Studies have shown that sitting all day actually takes years off your life! Set a timer for 55 minutes while you are working. When the alarm goes off, get up, walk around, drink water, and rest for 5 minutes.

- Take an hour one day a week to sit down and take a 360° look at the coming week. Notice where you are overcommitted or need help to get things done. Delegate to your spouse if you can. Say no if you need to. Having a clear picture of what's coming your way saves you tremendous amounts of stress and wasted mental energy. Make this a practice. It pays off big!

3. PASS! LET YOUR TEAM DO THEIR GENIUS WORK (SO YOU CAN DO YOURS)

One of the biggest obstacles for entrepreneurs is letting go. The truth is, you only have 24 hours in a day, so it's important to spend those precious minutes wisely. You can't be good at everything, so surround yourself with people who are great at the things that aren't your genius work.

Focus on things only you can do and delegate the rest.

This will free up time for you to take care of yourself. Yes, it will cost money, but there is nothing more expensive than bad health. If you do this well, you will be able to find an hour every day to engage in radical self-care!

4. PAUSE: CLEAN UP YOUR STRESS MESS

Everyone has stress, but for some people, it is chronic and persistent. This situation is like having a gang of thugs hanging out on the corner in your neighborhood. **Cortisol is the ringleader of the rogue band of bad girls and plays havoc with your sleep and weight and causes long-term damage to every organ system in your body.** It's not a pretty sight.

Entrepreneurs are highly susceptible to chronic persistent stress because they often fail to establish clear boundaries around the demands of business. With a 9-to-5 job, it's much easier to leave your work at the workplace; it is not so simple if you are the owner of a business. Set boundaries for yourself and those around you. Learn when to say "no" to the demands and requests of others.

5. PREVENT: CREATE A HEALTH MAINTENANCE PLAN

Your car needs regular maintenance, and so do you. As a busy entrepreneur, it's easy to forget about routine healthcare needs.

However, you put yourself at unnecessary risk by not getting these simple tests when you need them. Make yourself a maintenance calendar and batch appointments together when you can in order to save time. Here's the bare minimum of what you need and when you need it:

- Blood pressure: yearly or more often if you are on treatment and not at goal

- Bone density: age 65 or earlier if you are at risk for osteoporosis

- Cholesterol: yearly or more often if you are on treatment and not at goal

- Colonoscopy: at age 50, then every 10 years unless you have risk factors for colon cancer

- Diabetes: get screened if your blood pressure is > 135/80 or you are on medication for blood pressure

- Mammogram: Every 2 years after age 50 (unless you are at increased risk for breast cancer)

- Pap test: Every 3 years as long as 3 tests 3 years in a row were normal

6. PARTICIPATE: YOU ARE NOT AN ISLAND

One of the dangers of an entrepreneurial life is isolation. If you're working from home (and your team is virtual), it's easy to never get out of your jammies. This is not good for your emotional health. Isolation can be a depression trigger, so it's important for entrepreneurs to be mindful of the potential effects that being alone for long periods of time can have and to deal with it on an ongoing basis.

Each week, schedule one networking opportunity and one "just for fun" lunch with a pal. If you're not sure where to look for networking opportunities, here are a few to check out:

- Business Networking International (BNI)
- Your local chamber of commerce

- Service Corps of Retired Executives (SCORE)
- Meet-up groups
- A Dining for Women chapter

7. PACE: IT'S A MARATHON, NOT A SPRINT

We live in a world where we want it all and we want it now. As entrepreneurs, the temptation is to fall into the trap of all-or-nothing thinking. This kind of thinking makes having your own business feel like running in molasses. No one succeeds overnight, and if you grind away full steam day after day, you will burn out and be robbed of any joy your work brings. Period.

Pace yourself. Everything you try in business is an experiment. Some things will work better than others. Allow yourself time to just be. Freedom and flexibility are benefits of entrepreneurship. See them for the gifts they are.

THE BOTTOM LINE

Focusing on one area of healthy living is better than nothing, but the truth is that creating good long-term health outcomes requires attention to the whole person—mind, body, and spirit. Try applying the same core principles to your health as you would to your business and structure your "plan for a healthier you" like a business plan: identify your desired outcome, set reasonable goals, and establish a clear path to achieve success. If you find that it's too tough to go it alone, consider finding an accountability partner or hiring a coach to help you get started.

Creating new habits takes time and a willingness to commit to consistency. This is where self-leadership is so important. The key to success is taking baby steps and giving yourself permission to be imperfect. No one gets it right all the time!

The payoff for creating a solid wellness foundation is huge. When you create a "good neighborhood" by maximizing your health and energy levels, you're then able to really focus on what you're wanting in your business and go farther faster!

EXERCISE: CREATE A WEEKLY GAME PLAN (THE GUIDELINES):

1. Schedule an hour to do this exercise.

2. Gather all calendars and information about kids' schedules for the coming week.

3. Choose one word that describes how you want to feel in the coming week (e.g., powerful, calm, healthy).

4. Decide on your top 3 priorities for the week.

5. Of those 3, decide which you'd be happiest crossing off the list if you can only do one thing.

6. Make a list of appointments, meetings you must attend, and kids' events. Is there anything you need to say "no" to in order to feel the word in #3?

7. Schedule exercise and fun.

8. Make a list of errands to run. Batch them by area of town. Delegate if possible.

9. Decide what's for dinner every night. Make the grocery list as you are doing this.

10. Feel a sense of relief knowing that you no longer have to think about any of this for a week!

Angelika Christie

Angelika Christie is a mother of 5 children, naturopath, energy healer, yoga/meditation instructor, best-selling author, transformational speaker, visionary, coach, and lover of all life. Her unique understanding of our soul power and inherent cellular intelligence is centered in all her teaching and programs. Angelika says: "The path to true power, happiness, and freedom lays in recognizing who you truly are." Angelika helps women fully step into their ageless beauty and highest expression for unlimited personal and business success.

www.freedomwhisperer.com

. . . .

Angelika and I share the power of motherhood, having had 4 children myself. She has a heart of gold. I didn't know Angelika before we came to work together on this project; she was referred to me by a trusted source and that source was absolutely right. Angelika lives in the Bahamas and, when you look at her picture, she looks like a ray of sunshine. So imagine what she can infuse in her work with her clients!

Thank you, Angelika, for being a true light in this world. I know you'll be one in this book....

{ LESSON 5 }

KICK YOUR FEAR OF AGING
by Angelika Christie

There is one fear in particular that we grapple with—no, not even ladies in "high heels" are spared: It is the fear of aging. If you are still a spring chicken (in other words, if you have not reached at least your third decade), you might want to let your mom read this chapter.

Fear seems to be our natural companion in many areas of our lives. The most talked about fears that even female high achievers often struggle with include:

- Fear of the unknown
- Fear of re-creating yourself
- Fear of loneliness
- Fear of disease
- Fear of death

As we have limited space here, I will share with you my juiciest tips. You can start implementing them right away so you never lose your feminine magnetism, youth, and energy no matter how many candles might start to crowd your birthday cakes.

I know that the race against the clock had become a shared experience. Unless you have lived under a rock or on a remote island away from the hustle and bustle of modern life, you know and feel the time squeeze in many areas of your life. One thing we all have in common, no matter what your profession, talent, looks, genes, race, or color of your skin might be is that we age from moment to moment. You are likely thinking, "Oh no! I don't want to hear that." I understand, but it's true. The attention you give to dream up and manifest your perfect life applies even more to your physical body. After all, it is the vehicle that carries your excellent mind, your passionate desires for success, and your high soaring spirit out into the world, every day, from morning until night, in perpetual cycles of days, weeks, months, and years.

So here you are in your amazing body that your spirit/soul has chosen for this lifetime. Let me remind you that God and your soul made no mistake with you. In other words, you have everything that you would ever need—and even more—for an extraordinary life. You might be asking "Me? An extraordinary life?" Yes, you! You are not made for mediocrity. Did you know that it is easier to live a high-energy life than a low-energy or ordinary one?

You are a symphony of dancing light and energy, so your natural state is vibrant, radiant, and magnetic—that is, unless you dim your life-force with unhealthy choices and habits that you might have picked up and adapted to at some point in your life. Let's get rid of any heavy and unnecessary load that you might be carrying in your body. Are there "cobwebs" in your habitual thinking that negatively affect your emotions?

There may be a lot of uncertainty in some areas of your life, but the care of your physical, mental, and spiritual body as a holistic entity has not changed. Quite the opposite; the crazier the outer life becomes, the more we need to understand how to care for ourselves.

As we discovered earlier, your body's natural state subsists in high energy, vibrant health, and energetic creativity. Are you ready to re-claim or preserve this perfect state well into whatever age you can envision yourself in the future?

After decades of caring for my clients by designing their personalized diet feasting to radiant health, what lights me up is ageless beauty. It shows when you know who you are. I give you a glimpse here on how to stay youthful, healthy, and magnetic no matter how many years the calendar shows. I know how. I live it daily. Although I may be already quite a bit older than you are, I still have young men trying to pick me up. I don't say this because I love it, but because it shows that I still have "it" and I will keep "it" to the last day of my life.

I am not perfect, yet I am perfect in my imperfection—and so are you. If you feel radiant, energetic, magnetic, and inspired most of the time, congratulations! Just keep on doing what you have done to feel that way. But be aware that it is easier to feel that way when you are still in your 40s. Soon thereafter, you just have to pay more attention as the years race by you. Don't miss the early warning signs your body gives you; listen and understand her language when she knocks to get your attention about an internal stress/disease.

Can I share a secret with you? You can re-design everything in your life, including how your body looks and feels. How long does it take to change your body? It depends. But letting go of old habits and integrating new and superior ones actually takes a moon cycle. For simplicity and staying in alignment with the subtitle of this beautiful book, let's go with 30 days.

I am not asking you to just change, but to **transform** your life.

When you reach a crossroads or hit a wall in your business or personal life, changing things around a bit or adjusting to a changing situation might be "kicking the can down the street." Your strength and power rest in becoming pre-active, asking the right questions, and listening deeply to your body's inherent wisdom.

Basically, we encounter two trends in every future event. Some are hard trends and some are soft trends. Let me give you an example:

A hard trend:

You will age. Every moment moves along a linear progression toward a **certain** outcome.

A soft trend:

Although you will age, you can stay healthy, sexy, magnetic, fulfilled, and creative, depending on how well you take care of yourself.

You can modify almost everything by being wise, smart, and pre-active. If you are sure about something in the future, you can prepare intelligently. Once you see what is real and what is an illusion, you will be way ahead of most people. You will become fearless. This is true for your personal and business life.

Here is what I want you to do right now:

1. Buy yourself the most beautiful and sexy looking journal.

2. Give it a catchy name—after all, it is your very personal journal.

3. Schedule at least 15 minutes twice daily for reflection and discovery.

For the next least 30 days, write in your journal about your progress on the following exercises. No time? Schedule time. One of my favorite "Kick in the Butt" quotes is "If not now, when? If not you, who?"

Ready? **Let's do it...**

On the first page, create a written **commitment** that you date and sign. Read it every day!

Divide the next 30 days into 4 weeks.

WEEK ONE: GETTING TO KNOW AND LOVE YOUR BODY

Take a bit of extra time in the bathroom.

1. When you look into the mirror, don't look at what is wrong, but look into your eyes and really see yourself. Gaze a bit longer and smile at who you see.

2. Do about 20 squats (hold on to the basin). Laugh when you come up.

3. Stretch your legs by putting one at the time on your ledge bathtub and bringing your nose close to your knee.

4. Use your toothbrush with the other hand as well as your

comb. This grows millions of neurons in your brain.

5. Squeeze and stop the flow of urine as many times as possible—also known as Kegel exercises.

6. Feel the water on your skin when you shower; be sensuous.

WEEK TWO: FEEDING YOUR BODY WHAT SHE NEEDS

1. Reduce sugars and simple starches each day more and more.

2. Once a week, have only raw veggies and some fruit, but lots of water and tea.

3. Be aware if food makes you tired or energizes you; look for food allergies.

4. Adjust food intake according to your level of activity.

WEEK THREE: MOVING YOUR BODY THE WAY SHE LOVES IT

1. Your body needs to move, stretch, and hold her own weight.

2. Get out of breath at least once daily (sex counts), and mix it up with:

    ▪ Dancing

    ▪ Swimming

    ▪ Yoga

    ▪ Pilates

    ▪ Tennis

    ▪ Jogging

    ▪ Golf

WEEK FOUR: TAKING CARE OF YOUR EMOTIONAL AND SPIRITUAL NEEDS

1. Wake up with a big smile. Don't rush. Feel gratitude for your life and excitement for a brand new day.

40

2. Go outside barefoot and see the sun rise (if possible.) Meditate/pray.

3. Learn how to breathe for energy, relaxation, and healing.

4. Make a new friend each week, give something away, or pay it forward.

5. Help somebody succeed. Be generous; it will come back 1000 fold.

6. Listen more and talk less. Smile more and be patient. Take time to reflect.

7. Read or listen to something that inspires you for 30 minutes each day.

8. Witness yourself with humor.

9. Forgive.

Write in your journal daily, reflect, and witness your fear of aging disappear.

Dorothy-Inez Del Tufo

Dorothy-Inez, Minister of Beauty, is a Hollywood-trained makeup artist and visibility mentor. She is passionate about teaching women how to align who they are with how they show up by helping them connect with their inner and outer beauty! Dorothy-Inez works with soul-inspired, heart-centered women who are ready to release their irresistible brand of beauty in photos, video and at live events. She is honored to serve her country as the spouse of a U.S. Army Captain, which expands her reach to women around the world.

www.dorothyinez.com

www.facebook.com/celebrityentrepreneur

www.twitter.com/dorothyinez

www.pinterest.com/dorothyinez

. . . .

I met Dorothy-Inez for this project through a mutual and loving friend. Dorothy-Inez is a Visual Brand Mentor who specializes in makeup artistry. Over the past 15 years in the industry, she has worked with many high profile television and fashion celebrities. So, she is no stranger to helping women look and feel fabulous!

I am amazed by how gifted she is with helping women shine in their own beauty. I really love her title "Minister of Beauty". I've learned her work isn't just about makeup, it's about inspiring women to transform their beauty from the inside-out.

Many thanks, Dorothy-Inez, for sharing your beauty with our readers.

{ LESSON 6 }

REVEAL YOUR BRAND WITH BEAUTY
by Dorothy-Inez Del Tufo

· ·

I haven't always felt beautiful. In fact, I once felt ugly on the inside. My story is much like the stories of many other women—maybe even you. Although I receive many compliments about my outer appearance, it's my inner beauty that I am grateful for the most.

Let me share with you a little about me. I was abandoned by my mother as a child, left to believe I could only count on myself, causing me to feel angry and very lonely inside. I was also told countless times that I was overweight, too talkative, and selfish, which slowly shattered my self-worth. Although I had a low self-esteem on the inside, I became a master of outwardly appearing strong and confident. At a young age, I quickly learned to gain control of my life by managing how I looked to others and becoming a lifetime overachiever. It wasn't until I found the courage to begin my journey to self-love that I discovered the real meaning of beauty. There was a time I had to survive, but today I choose to thrive and live a beautiful life.

In 2006, after finally graduating from college, I made one of the biggest decisions of my life: At the age of 40, I left my high-paying corporate career to pursue my childhood dream of becoming a makeup artist and image consultant. Talk about scary. I had heard my hero, motivational speaker Les Brown, ask one too many times, "What hopes and dreams have you put on the shelf of your heart?" With great passion, he would say, "The richest place on the planet is the graveyard because so many people die with their ideas, never bringing them to life." The thought of dying and not knowing if I could have made it did something to my soul. I just could not be comfortable wondering any longer. I had to know if I could make it and if I had what it would take to live my "impossible" dream.

After nearly a decade of watching the video "This is Your Decade," I finally "heard" and understood was Les Brown was saying. I didn't want to have any part of making the graveyard any richer. I didn't want to be one of those people who would sit out on the porch rocking back and forth at age 60 or 70, saying "I wish I would have tried _____" or "I wonder what if _____." I always inspired the people I led to be their best self and go for their dreams, yet I was not leading by example. Like many women, I was stuck in fear. There was always this recording of my concerned father's voice in my mind, saying on a repeat cycle "There ain't no money in beauty. You need something stable that's going to bring in money." That voice kept me from ever having to depend on anyone and from ever taking any chances. Like many parents of my generation, my father was only looking out for me based on what he had been taught. The time had come for me to fulfill my life's purpose of helping women look and feel beautiful from the inside out.

So often women get caught up in the outside beauty or the inside beauty, not realizing that beauty is a total package. You cannot be "beauty-full" if you are not whole inside and out. Beauty is not just about putting a bunch of makeup on your face, nor is it walking around saying, "I love who I am." The truth is the outside is a direct reflection of what is going on inside. When we love someone, we demonstrate that love by giving them our time, affection, words of encouragement, gifts, and more, right? Let me ask, are you showing yourself that kind of unconditional love? Be honest. I cannot tell you how many women tell me "I don't do my makeup because I don't have time," "It's too much work," "I hate the way I look," "I'm too old," "Too tired," or "My partner/spouse doesn't like me to wear makeup." The list goes on. Can I just say that it breaks my heart? Like I said, I didn't always feel beautiful, but when I embraced the fact that I am a beautifully and wonderfully made masterpiece from God and that I have a purpose in this life, my self-image was transformed. The same goes for you! You, my sister, are not here by accident, but on purpose.

When you truly love you and who you are, you will make time to beautify and adorn your temple with clothing and makeup that communicates who you are; you will eat right and take care of your body because those are all acts of love. The love you feel for yourself is then communicated in who you are and how you show up in life and in your business. Have you ever met a woman who was beautiful on the outside, but when she opened her mouth nothing but ugly came out? That's an example of a woman who does not love herself, and she uses makeup to camouflage the hurt and insecurity. My greatest hope is that all women discover just how beautiful they are inside and out. When you begin to truly stand in your total beauty, you will feel empowered and confident, experience abundance, and be able to attract the relationships you desire personally and professionally. Everything around you will begin to transform as you begin to live from a place of "beauty-full" love for yourself.

So, let me share with you some steps to begin living a "beauty-full" love of yourself. Before you begin, find a beautiful journal to write about your journey as you reconnect, restore, and revitalize yourself!

STEP ONE: DEVELOP A BEAUTIFUL MINDSET

We have all heard it: "What you think about, you bring about." Everything we manifest in our lives starts with a thought. In your journal, write the answers to the following questions. Be honest and real. If you cry, let it out!

1. What negative thoughts do I have about myself in terms of beauty? (e.g., Not pretty enough. I look old, too fat. I don't like my nose, my skin, my eyes.) Be honest and list them all. No one is going to see this but you.

2. What negative thoughts do I have about who I am? (e.g., I am not good enough. I am not important. I am not valuable. No one loves me.)

3. Is my thinking based on fact? Does this thinking help me achieve my goals? Does this thinking help me to feel the way I want to feel? If you answered "no" to all of these, then write an "I Am" statement to replace the current negative mantra you have been feeding yourself. For example, "I am not good enough" becomes "I am good enough." Write the statement on notecards or sticky notes and place them where you will see them every day. It's about replacing the old mantras with the truth mantras.

STEP TWO: RECONNECT WITH SOURCE AND SELF

This step is probably the greatest gift you can give to yourself. For me, this source is God, but use your own higher source. When you connect with God, you will discover who you were designed to be; something inside shifts as you realize you were born to shine. You are a light in the world with your message and being. I would like to challenge you to give yourself the sacred gift of time starting with 10 minutes per day. In those 10 minutes, consider the following to help you connect with God and the self:

1. Sing or listen to music: Music and singing are fantastic ways of connecting to God. Create a playlist on your iPod/MP3 player of songs that really minister to your spirit. A couple of artists I find to be empowering for women are: India Arie, Karen Drucker, and Whitney Houston.

2. Dance: Sometimes we don't have the words. By dancing, we can express our emotions and release them through body movement. A good book to read on this is called Sweat Your Prayers.

3. Traditional meditation: Quieting your mind can be very challenging. Guided meditation can help you develop your ability to quiet your mind. If you find yourself getting distracted, focus on your breath, a mantra, or a scripture verse or voice your intention for your quiet time. Find what works for you within the bonds of your spiritual beliefs.

Choose one or try all of these forms of spiritual connection. Write in your journal daily to express any insights you might discover during this time with yourself. Be conscious of patterns or messages you hear in your spirit—it's that small, still voice. Even if you think it is you, write it down. Then come back and reflect on your journey.

STEP THREE: UNLEASH YOUR GORGEOUS FACTOR (G-FACTOR)

This is the final key to unlocking the door to your "beauty-full" self. Your brand of beauty speaks to the world before you ever do. Your beauty and adornments communicate messages about your self-esteem, values, quality of work, attention to detail, and more.

Our G-factor is what initially attracts others to us; what you say is secondary. Studies have shown that as much as 85% of what you say is in what you don't say. In other words, your image is constantly broadcasting a message without you ever saying a word. What message do you want to broadcast? Are you on the right frequency? Here are some ways to transform your G-factor today:

1. Smile: A smile is a universal language. It welcomes others from a distance and makes you more approachable.

2. Wear some makeup to polish up your look: It can help you look more vibrant and put together. According to Newsweek, studies show that women who are perceived as attractive earn 4% more than their less attractive counterparts. Now that can add up!

3. Enlist the help of a beauty or visual brand mentor: A mentor can help you discover your best colors, style personality, haircuts, makeup, and more. When you have a beauty brand mentor, you are able to bring your total beauty to the world and make a great first impression.

Challenge: Create a beauty brand board, which is very similar to a vision board except you use style and beauty magazines. Cut out pictures and words that communicate your story. Glue the pictures and words on a poster board in collage style. Then enlist the help of a professional or a trusted friend to help you create the look. Don't try to do it alone because your past stories may hinder your growth in this area. You need someone who is committed to helping you experience transformation.

In closing, remember that you are a unique and valuable creation. You are a one-of-a-kind masterpiece, which means there is no one like you. Don't let fear, your past, or your thinking hold you back from living your best and most beautiful life. Give yourself permission to shine and revel in your beauty. When you do, I promise everything else in your life will transform.

Noni Boon

Noni Boon holds a diploma in arts, a certificate in holistic counseling, and a certificate in communication skills and is an accredited intuitive consultant. With her knowledge of art and life, Noni developed a series of five simple yet effective principles called "Life Design" that help people find their creative power, channel clear inspiration, and completely transform their lives for the better.

www.BiDesignCo.com

✉ **Mail@BiDesignCo.com**

🅕 **www.facebook.com/noniboon** or

🅕 **www.facebook.com/bidesignco**

. . . .

I'm so proud to know Noni. She is an example of walking the talk. Everything she helps her clients with is coming from that genuine place of experience. Very successful in her first business, she didn't hesitate to build a second one to fulfill a deep sense of helping others. I knew I wanted her to share her wisdom with you because she has so much to give.

Thank you, Noni, for trusting me with this project and for being the second person to say "Count me in."

{ LESSON 7 }

THE POWER BENEATH ME

by Noni Boon

. . . .

The wind of heaven is that which blows
between a horse's ears. ~Arabian proverb

On a cold winter's night, my husband and I joined some friends in attending the East Coast Championships, a horse show held at the Sydney Equestrian Centre, Horsley Park. At the time, I owned a former racehorse named Alobar, who I rescued from a property in Arcadia. Toward the end of the night, a horse was brought into the ring to compete for the Champion Arabian Warm-blood Gelding title. He was a large bay with jet black legs, perfect confirmation, and a small white star on his face. For me, it was love at first sight! I leaned in close to my husband and whispered in his ear, "I don't care what it takes, I have to have that horse!"

Oh So Sauvé was announced the 2004 Triple Crown Winner that night and, during the next two weeks, I convinced his reluctant owner to sell him to me. We eventually agreed on a price and, after purchasing a large horse float to transport him, I brought him home. My long journey had begun. I was about to learn a lot about horses and a lot about life at the same time. The partnership between woman and horse has to do with power and empowerment. I had successfully purchased a very powerful animal. I was about to become empowered. Having owned Alobar for one year and having taken riding lessons as a kid, I thought I knew how to ride quite well. Sauvé was about to teach me that I didn't have a clue and—for my own safety and sanity—I'd better learn fast.

After my first ride on Sauvé, I discovered that he was a step ahead of me. It hadn't taken him long to assess that I was a weak rider with not enough skill to handle his large mass and athletic ability. Without notice, Sauvé launched into a 180-degree turn in mid air, changing direction completely and then running off as if he knew it was bad! Caught unaware, I slid out of the saddle and rolled over to one side, catching my foot in the top strand of a wire fence. As Sauvé pulled away from me, my ankle was stretched and torn until I eventually hit the ground with a tremendous thud. After the initial shock, I collected myself up and slowly rose in agonizing pain. I limped sorely over to Sauvé, gathered up the reins, dragged over the mounting block, and pulled myself up into the saddle. I couldn't ride, but I was determined to sit there for just a few minutes so that Sauvé got the message that rides don't end this way.

Two weeks later, I saddled up my big brute and limped a kilometer down the road to where a riding teacher resided. I needed lessons— lots of them! Over the next four years, I had consistent riding lessons with various different instructors. For the first few months, every time I had to ride Sauvé, I was overcome with fear. I would hold the reins so tight that I ended up with blisters on my hands. I cringe now to think what that was doing to Sauvé's tender mouth. The first thing I learned was how to manage my fear. I learned that fear holds tight, paralyzing and crippling the process of trust and progress. Whatever is held too tight cannot flow and move with grace and ease. Over time, I learned to let go and maintain a contact built on trust and confidence. This allowed Sauvé to go on to the bit, flex at the poll, and relax into a submissive partnership with me.

The second thing I learned was that I needed to acquire new skills so that I could succeed as a rider and horse owner. I needed to develop my natural talent for riding and improve upon what I had in order to be able to go to the next level. I was willing to listen and learn. I drew all that I could from each and every lesson, taking on board what worked for me and passing over what didn't. I brought my own logic and common sense to my riding and started to create some confidence in my ability. No man is an island, and we need each other's help and expertise. I no longer hesitate to ask for help, and I have learned to reach out and ask for support and encouragement whenever I need it. The skills that I have gained as a rider help me immensely in my everyday life.

The third thing I learned was that to be assertive does not mean being offensive or aggressive. Sauvé is easily offended and very easily stressed. This has forced me to be patient, kind, and firm in how I ask him to perform. If I am aggressive or sharp with him, he tenses up, tucks in behind the bit, and moves like a stiff plank. Riding requires me to relax, sit quietly, and activate my intuition. Sauvé is extremely intuitive. He reads my mind and my body language. I only need to think canter, and he starts to canter. Sauvé is so sensitive to my body weight distribution that simply turning my head to the right while going over a jump alerts him to the fact that we turn right after the jump. He can feel the subtlest shift in my position or posture.

The fourth thing I learned was that I needed strength, fitness, and stamina along with knowing when to be quiet, relaxed, and peaceful. At times, opposing aids need to be used together in order to achieve a result. This is all about balance, timing, and feeling. In order to encourage Sauvé down on to the bit, I need to use forward-driving aids, being legs on, and half-halting the reins (meaning stop) at the same time. This collects him up into an outline and allows his back to rise, forcing him to use all of his muscles together. Too much of any one aid will ruin the outcome. I have learned how to use just enough drive, maintain control, and keep my eye on the goal, all at once. This is multi-tasking at its best, and it has been incredibly helpful in riding and in life.

The fifth thing I learned was to respond quickly. I had to hone my reflexes so that I could reward Sauvé within a split second of him performing correctly. The best reward I can give Sauvé is to be still and quiet on his back. The use of riding aids—being legs on tightly around his ribs, sometimes a spur, sometimes a whip—translates into something that prompts Sauvé to respond. Once he is responding appropriately, the prize for him is for me to take a portion of those aids off and stop bothering him. Of course, there is a fine line between taking too much off and stopping altogether and rewarding him by easing off just enough to feel good without completely abandoning the job.

The sixth thing I learned was about thoughts, words, and visualization. I had taken Suavé out to many jumping competitions over the years. We had never achieved a blue ribbon, which represents first place. This was a goal and a dream for me. The day before a competition last year, I decided to try something new. I actually allowed myself to win a blue ribbon in my thoughts and in my imagination. I closed my eyes and imagined the feeling of winning a blue ribbon. I spoke out loud to the universe, saying "I have worked hard for this; Sauvé and I deserve to win." I left it at that and went out to do my best. That day, I came home with a blue ribbon. To make it all sweeter, I had my baby boy on my hip when I collected it.

The seventh thing I learned was to work hard, commit to my success, and look for inspiration in those who have gone before me. I now have a vision board on my wall containing a picture of world champion show jumper Edwina Alexander. I look at that picture every day, and my riding continues to improve with ease. All I need to do is look at the picture and feel excited about becoming a better, more competent rider. It is so easy and effortless! I haven't yet attracted her Gucci contract, but I have thrown out all of my ripped jodhpurs!

If you haven't already done so, I encourage you to create a vision board. Simply use a piece of board, fix it to the wall, and attach pictures of people who inspire you, places you would like to go, the perfect home—anything at all that you would like to attract into your life. Look at that board once a day for a minute or two. That's all it takes to fire up the law of attraction.

Lillian Ogbogoh

Lillian Ogbogoh's work and passion in this life focus on empowering women. As the goddess creator, she enjoys guiding women to redefine their self-relationships and sensuality, taking them on a journey to rediscover the desirable, delicious, sensuous, and femifierce women that they are. Her work has led her to speak both internationally as well as locally in the UK; she has spoken in Europe and the Cayman Islands. She is also a radio chat show host of a show called Waking Passions, where she gets to interview amazing people on various journeys in their lives.

www.LillianOgbogoh.com

✉ **Info@Lillianogbogoh.com**

✉ **Goddesscreator@lillianogbogoh.com**

🐦 **www.twitter.com/lillianogbogoh**

• •

Before working with Lillian on this project, I had the chance to speak with her over Skype, and it was a delight. She is vibrant, brilliant, and amazing all at once. As women, we've got to own our sensuality, which can serve us in our business—why not? We were given some attribute so it could better serve us, right? And Lillian is a wonderful teacher in this regard. Let your true self shine and allow Lillian to gently guide you.

Thanks again, Lillian, for our wonderful conversation. Soon we'll get the chance to drink tea together in London—I can't wait. You are a true Goddess, from the inside out.

{ LESSON 8 }

IMPACT YOUR BUSINESS BY DISCOVERING THE WISDOM OF YOUR SENSUAL GODDESS

by Lillian Ogbogoh

. . . .

Now you are probably wondering what the heck the sensual goddess can teach you about impacting your business. For some of you, you might be glancing back at the dustcover to see when you ventured into the land of New Age mumbo-jumbo. But if you give me your attention for this chapter, I will take you on a journey that will show you the gifts of discovering the wisdom of your sensual goddess and the impact that it will have on your business.

Many women have divorced their yummy, juicy, sensual selves from their day-to-day lives, confining them to the bedroom and in the most extreme cases from their lives entirely. So we will start this journey with an introduction to the sensual goddess.

When we think of the sensual goddess, many think of the Greek goddess Aphrodite, who is considered the epitome of beauty, femininity, and all things pleasurable. According to her birth myth, she emerged fully grown from the spot in the Aegean Sea where her father Uranus's severed genitals had been thrown. She represents the perfect union of the feminine and the masculine in raw sensuality and sexuality. Yet this description of the sensual goddess is only half the story. Jean Shinoda Bolen, the Jungian analyst, refers to Aphrodite as the transformative alchemical goddess as she alone had the magical powers of transformation that could cause gods and mortals alike to do her biding and the ability to cast spells that caused mortals and deities alike to fall in love and conceive brand new lives. She once turned a statue into a living woman for Pygmalion after he fell in love with the statue.

Aphrodite embodies all that is sensual, creative, passionate, and juicy; she is open and playful, tapping into the delicious yumminess that lives at the core of the sensual side that makes up the feminine essence. She had a clear understanding of her own power, purpose, and desires; she never apologized for what she wanted and found ways to manifest her desire into being. I guess you can say her mantra was "what Aphrodite wants, Aphrodite gets."

Aphrodite was more than her charms, looks, and alchemy. She had the power of influence over others; she possessed the amazing ability of concentrated attention. She knew how to own the limelight, yet she had ways of drawing people into that light and making them feel unique and extraordinary. When she decided to turn her charms on a person, she acted as if that person were the sole person in the world. She made it her mission to unearth what others' true desires were and then grant them.

Now I know you are thinking that this is a fascinating Jungian breakdown of the Greek goddess, but you fail to see how this helps you to impact and grow your business exponentially. The Greek goddess was the archetypal embodiment of all that is sensual, powerful, and transformative in every woman. If you go over her story again, you will see the clues are there for creating enormous change in your business and life without sacrificing your femininity or abusing your masculine side, which leads to burn out, exhaustion, fatigue, overwhelm, and feelings of being over-worked and underappreciated.

CLUE 1: MASTERING THE ART OF YOUR FULL FEMININE PRESENCE

What is mastering the art of your full feminine presence? Think of Aphrodite's story: She always showed up in a room with the ability to captivate and be magnetic. When she entered a room, there was never any doubt as to who she was. She was magnetic and fully present, drawing everyone to her with very little effort and great ease. She had the ability to make others feel important and special in a way that held others enthralled; that was part of her power. She understood how to wield the full force of her feminine essence. This clue is very vital for us as women in all aspects of our lives, but especially so in our businesses.

When women fully entered the business and corporate world starting in the early 1980s, they had to conform to the system at hand, disconnecting themselves totally from their feminine ways. These corporate women chose to play the men at their own games, feeling that for them to become successful, they had to become honorary men. The power suits, power plays, and lone wolf stance of everybody was competition reflected in their state of being, which left most of these women unsatisfied, fatigued, and ill to boot.

Every woman is gifted with a feminine presence. Have you ever been at a party where a woman walks in and without saying a word is instantly noticed by everyone for all the right reasons? There is an air of confidence about her that draws others to her like a bee to nectar. It's attractive and magnetizing. Yet at the same party there will be women who won't be remembered even if they had hung neon signs around their necks. Your full feminine presence is about being centered and present in your body, knowing the impact you have on others when you walk into a room and how you show up and shine free of your gremlins (self-doubts). Aphrodite would never allow her gremlins to stand in her way of showing up. She learned to fully embrace her shadow sides, her gremlins and self- doubts, so when she does show up, she does so without apologizing for being there. For some women, when they show up, they bring their gremlins to the business meeting, sales event, or networking occasions. They totally cover up that vivacious, juicy femifierce energy under their shadows and gremlins. They look like they are apologizing for being in the room; their bodies look like they are trying to hide in plain view or in some extreme cases trying to vanish completely.

So when a woman embodies her full feminine presence, her magnetism increases, which overflows into every area of her life. It's about knowing how and what your body is saying about you: Is it speaking yummy sensual woman who acknowledges her own presence and worth or is it speaking in the language of self-doubt? You should use your body the same way a first chair of the Philharmonic orchestra will use and see a Stradivarius violin: as a magnificent masterpiece that creates magic whenever it's played.

Get to know what your powerful pose is as a sensual being; without mimicking Tom, Dick, and Harry, learn how to master the "I'm in the room and see me" stance that is graceful, authentic for you, and subtle. Have you ever noticed that woman who looks like she is trying too hard to be seen? That is not the authentic feminine presence; that is someone trying to be in her powerful pose man style, stuffed into a female body. What works for men in their majestic presence will not work for us. Learn to own your space when you walk into a room; make eye contact and flash that megawatt smile on someone to captive and magnetize them instantly. The only way you are going to master this is to practice it on your own in front of a mirror and with trusted friends to see how your body looks when you enter a room, sit, and stand. Do you look like you are playing at being the invisible woman or the one who looks self-assured, confident, and approachable with your femifierceness intact?

Sensual Goddess Lesson 1:

When you feel a case of the gremlins or are having an off day, remember the golden rule of "faking it until you make it." Think of the movie *Avatar* and imagine you are the sensual goddess who will enthrall and captivate whomever she connects with wherever you go on that day and see yourself stepping into this amazing version of you and taking her for a test drive.

CLUE 2: KNOW AND OWN YOUR DESIRE

Aphrodite always knew what she wanted and took great pride in manifesting it into her reality. She never apologized for her desires; in fact, she owned them and relished in having them. For some women, we have been programmed to disown and disavow our desires; if we did speak them into being, it is always accompanied with a justification or an apology. For these women, when they chose to enter the arena of birthing a business, this instantly created a conflict

59

within them in the areas of money, their vision, and desires of what they can and can't do.

You have some women saying things like "Well I want to make money but it's not important—I don't want to be seen as greedy, I don't want to stand out because I don't want to come across as better than anyone. I want to make money so I can help others and support a charity. No, it's not about the money, it's about the service." We cloak our desires in self-effacing justifications and apologies. What is wrong with wanting to make money for you and buy that luxury item you have been secretly yearning for? What will happen if you spoke your true desire, unwrapped, without apologizing for it out loud?

Most of us have come across the laws of attraction in one form or another and understand the power of manifestation, goal setting, and vision boarding for our business. Yet we never put 2+2 together to understand why disowning and disavowing our desires keeps our business small and contracted. Quite frankly, we are sending out mixed messages. If you are one of these women, you will never get what you don't really want!

Sensual Goddess Lesson 2:

To grow your business from where it is right now and create massive changes, it is time to look at your desires and why you are in business: Are they wrapped in apologies and justifications or do you really own them? Are you ready to say loud and proud as the sensual goddess "I want this for me"? It's time to put your order into your divine or universe, saying openly and unapologetically without any justifications, "I want this [whatever your desire may be] just because I deserve it."

CLUE 3: USING SEDUCTIVE COMMUNICATION FOR INFLUENCE:

This is the final clue on how to impact your business by discovering the wisdom of your sensual goddess. When Aphrodite wanted to influence mortals and immortals alike, she was adept at using seductive communication. She did not lay out commands and orders; she understood the principle of catching more flies with honey than vinegar. When she set in motion her plan to get Paris to pick her in a contest between herself and two other goddesses, she did it by offering him his heart's desire. She had ways of drawing people in and making them feel unique and extraordinary, while getting them on her side without the need of a single command. She discovered what they wanted and gave it to them; they in turn carried out her desires without question. Imagine how powerful this ability is! You could use the power of your seductive communication to get new clients and close that negotiation deal without making the other party feel as if they had lost something. You could get your team highly motivated and eager to complete the tasks you have set for them with flourish. What benefit will that have on your business?

You could say that Aphrodite had a grasp on how to win friends and influence people; she knew the 3 W's behind influencing anyone: the why, what, and who. She always knew why she was focusing on the person she was engaging with. Whether it was to get Paris to give her the golden apple or to get Persephone to hide Adonis in Hades, she knew why she wanted the ultimate outcome.

Before she communicated with any mortal, she was also clear what she wanted from them; in other words, she had a crystal clear idea on what she intended her outcome to be. She made it her mission to know who she was dealing with at all times, what they needed and desired, and what secret yearning they had. To simplify, she made it about them by discovering who they were, and she was able to get what she wanted by meeting their desires first. She did so by casting the light on them, instead of coming into the room and making it all about her and what she wanted. She would focus entirely on who they were by asking them about themselves and unearthing what made them tick and what made their world come alive. In your day-to-day business life, what would you gain if you had the power to captive, magnetize, and influence people with unbelievable ease and grace, creating a positive outcome for you and those you encountered?

Sensual Goddess Lesson 3:

Become skilled at seductive communication by following the simple rules to understand that you catch more flies with honey than vinegar. Know your 3 W's—why, what, and who—whenever you are engaging a new client, a potential joint venture partner, or even a loyal client. When you sit around that table, work to ensure that your desires are met as well as having theirs met too. If it's impossible to have their desires met, make sure they don't walk away feeling like they have lost.

So put the wisdom of your sensual goddess into action next time you are attending a meeting, networking event, or even boardroom event. Remember your full feminine presence, speak up for your desires without apologizing for them, and remember the rules of seductive communication. Understand that you catch more flies with honey than vinegar, and know your 3 W's: the why, what, and who.

Being your full sensual goddess takes practice. The easiest way to embody everything about your sensual goddess is to play make believe. Think about the movie Avatar and create your own image of your sensual goddess self—the one who is amazing, captivating, and yummy, the one that will enthrall and charm everyone you connect with wherever you go. Imagine that you are putting all of these delicious qualities that allow you to connect to your sensual goddess into a version of you; the more you add the qualities you want to see, the more this image of you begins to glow and shine. Once she is full to the brim with all the yumminess you can muster, envision yourself stepping into this amazing version of you just like in the movie and taking her for a test drive. Let her be you at your next meeting that you are nervous about or when you have to give that public speaking presentation.

Angela Raspass

Angela Raspass is a Compass and Catalyst for Entrepreneurs. She brings clarity, new possibilities and fresh ideas to inspire and empower women who are motivated to reach their full potential through her marketing and mindset work at **www.angelaraspass. com.** Angela has over 25 years' experience in sales and marketing in the corporate world and is also a business consultant and franchise owner. She adores her kids and husband, loves reading, and plays soccer on the weekend with little skill but great enthusiasm!

Download your free copy of "The Lighthouse Effect"—4 steps for gaining clarity and losing that feeling of being overwhelmed—at **www.angelaraspass.com.**

www.facebook.com/angelaraspass

au.linkedin.com/in/angelaraspass/

http://pinterest.com/angelaraspass/

. . . .

Angela is a gem from Australia. She runs the show at home like at work. She is a mum and a CEO. She represents the perfect example, showing that you can have it all—even if you can't do it all by yourself. She is very warm and eager to help. I met her for this project, and I'm so glad I did.

Thank you, Angela, for your willingness to jump into gear and make it all happen in a short period of time.

{ LESSON 9 }

YOUR LIGHTHOUSE AND YOUR ANCHOR
by Angela Raspass

. . . .

Have you ever felt adrift, holding that feeling close to your chest as you move through your life, each day feeling a lot like the last? Has that negative voice inside of your head delivered consistent judgment that you are too this or too that or not enough—not smart enough, unique enough, talented enough, or thin enough?

Perhaps you've buried these emotions, pushed them down with food, shopping, alcohol, or another substance or activity. Maybe you have consistently put your needs and desires behind others as a mother, a co-worker, a wife, or a friend. If you've fallen into this habit, there's a very good chance that when someone asks you "so, what do you like to do?", you find it difficult to truly answer from your heart because you've lost touch of what brings you joy—what lights you up, inspires you, and fills you with excitement.

I'm not suggesting that your days are all bleak, but I do believe that many of us hold ourselves back from what we are really capable of achieving or from doing what would truly make our hearts sing in life and in our businesses. There can be a great many reasons why: concerns about being judged, fear of risk or failure, a level of comfort with where you are—why challenge what seems to be working ok? Or perhaps you have tried—perhaps often—to take yourself and your business to the next level and it hasn't worked, so you feel overwhelmed and discouraged and haven't tried again.

We all know that we only have this one life to live, yet we find ourselves settling for less than we could achieve, embrace, and enjoy if we could shrug off the fears, stop comparing our insides to other people's outsides, dismiss the harsh self-judgment, and just leap off the mountain, confident that we would grow our wings on the way down.

I have felt many of these negative emotions and allowed them to divert me away from reaching for my own true potential for several years. But with help, I escaped, getting back on track, and my life is so very different now. I'd like to share a little of my journey with you and how it has shaped me and my outlook on life as well as the way I have grown my businesses as a result.

I am fortunate to now be absolutely on purpose in a business that aligns with my skills and passions. I have developed a number of tools that I share with other entrepreneurial women as they break through their own challenges. Together, we focus on developing clarity and self-belief before we turn our attention to marketing their businesses. Although I am a strategic marketer by trade, with more than 20 years of experience, I know firsthand that without true clarity and a positive mindset, all the marketing in the world will not deliver the business success that you desire and deserve. I am a compass and a catalyst for entrepreneurs, and this work deeply satisfies, excites, and energizes me. I want this delicious, powerful feeling for you too!

But it wasn't always like this, and it took me awhile to get here. Allow me to rewind a few years…

To the outside world I presented a pretty consistent picture of how a good life should be. I had a lovely home in a leafy suburb and a successful marketing career in the corporate world. My husband and I welcomed two children—a son and then a daughter—who joined two sons from his first marriage. I took some time out when they were born and then took over the marketing of my husband's business before launching my own consultancy, working with small business owners. Everything was just peachy, right?

No. Inside I felt flat, unhappy, and unfulfilled—and enormously guilty for feeling that way. I could not define exactly what was wrong with me, because there had to be something wrong with me, surely? My life ticked all the boxes, what right did I have to feel the way I was feeling? Why did I feel like such a fake, that I wasn't good enough?

I knew without a doubt that everyone else was far more talented and deserving and that I could not and would not achieve more with my life. Naturally I didn't share these feelings with anyone. I was ashamed. Instead, I submerged them behind a mask of bright confidence and positivity and just got on with it.

I was acutely afraid that the façade would eventually begin to crack and that the real me would be revealed. I began to form a new habit, winding down with a few drinks at the end of the day to deal with this feeling of disquiet. This "relaxation technique" gradually began to play a larger role in quieting the doubts, turning down the volume on the negative voice, and filling the hole inside me.

I now know I am not alone when it comes to looking for a solution outside of myself to address what is essentially an inside problem. At the beginning, this solution seemed so innocent, so soporific, the stress and doubt and problems melted away. I felt better, so it made perfect sense to seek this benign comforter more. But by my mid 30s, it was no longer working for me and, speaking honestly, my liquid companion took a pretty nasty toll on me spiritually and emotionally.

Fortunately my wake-up call came in time, and I reached out and received amazing support to find my way out of the deep hole I had fallen into. Today my life is so completely different than how it was that I often find myself a little in awe. Please allow me to be clear here: I live in the same house with the same husband and children, I am still in the same industry, and I definitely can have crappy days like we all do! However, a significant change has taken place primarily on the inside. The fear, self-doubt, sadness, and dissatisfaction have been replaced with courage, clarity, and a healthy self-esteem.

So how did I get from where I was to where I am today? With a fairly simple set of tools that I believe are universal in their application and particularly important to female entrepreneurs. I'd like to share a few of them with you.

We are in a golden era now. More women than ever before are starting their own businesses. We are choosing flexibility and freedom and the desire to do things we are passionate about over the previous corporate ladder alternative. This is particularly true when we have children. We are entering the Experts Age, where the power of the internet and all of the tools it provides us with have removed geographic and economic boundaries that previously kept the title of business owner or entrepreneur for those who had vast finances to draw upon. It is infinitely exciting!

However, research tells us that too many women are not reaching their full potential in business. We are not owning our self-worth, and this is likely to be a key reason why many of us do not generate the levels of satisfaction and income that are possible and that make this entrepreneurial journey the exciting and invigorating adventure it can be. A recent *Wall Street Journal* report found that, although more women business owners are raking in the seven-digit revenues, these high-earners account for just 1.8% of all female business owners. Less than 20% of us generate revenues in excess of $100,000. Our average is $60,000.

In my reckoning, this is definitely not okay!

I'm not suggesting that all of us are itching to break the "magical million dollar barrier." One of the beauties of being an entrepreneur is being able to define success on our own terms, which extends far past a simple financial result. Yet I do believe that given the time, effort, and sheer passion we invest into our businesses as well as the value that we bring to our clients, we should be richly rewarded.

As a marketer, I do know that having the right strategy is, of course, vital. Taking focused, consistent action so that this strategy is executed is also paramount for success. But as a marketer, an entrepreneur, and an individual who has experienced a significant mindset shift and change in business direction, I am convinced that there are other key pieces of the puzzle that must be in place beforehand.

The starting points are clarity and self-belief. In the entrepreneurial sense, the mix of clarity and self-belief is a unique-to-you patchwork quilt of several factors, including:

- **An honest, no-holding-back vision of where you want to take your business:** Try putting yourself forward in time, say 3-5 years, and looking back at your perfect business and describing what it looks like in great detail: staff, business model, products and services, revenue, clients, location, the hours you work—everything that is important to you and you truly desire in your working life.

- **A confident claim on your personal flair and the way you deliver what it is that you do:** Whatever industry you are in, there is competition—and that's fine. Focus on developing an abundance perspective: There is more than enough business for us all. But make sure you have your own recipe and flavor. Define and claim what makes you you and what specific outcomes you deliver to your clients. Then communicate that boldly and consistently so that your tribe, your prospects, and the people you are meant to serve are drawn to you.

- **The development of a rich description and an understanding of who your clients are to be:** Who do you simply love working with and in what ways? Although I built my marketing business from $1,000 a month at the dining room table to multiple six figures in an office with a team, I could no longer ignore the fact that there was something else that I really wanted to do: shift my focus from serving businesses in the agency model of multiple services to serving female entrepreneurs with marketing strategy and mindset work. If you look deeply inside, would you make a change?

- **An exploration of what the concept of a higher power means to you—the universal flow, God, or whatever name or word resonates with you.** Tune into this power on a daily basis through meditation and writing a simple gratitude list. Have clear intentions for what you want to achieve in your business and put in your best efforts, but release yourself from the expectations of specific outcomes. Freedom, ease, and acceptance that you are enough just as you are all lay within this approach, I promise.

- **A strong challenge of that voice in your head.** Take note of what it says, writing the assertions down and really looking at them. Recognize that there is no reason why you should regard this voice as worthy of your attention. Who is to say that it is right? Where is the evidence that you cannot achieve what you want to achieve? Write down statements that directly contradict those negative words. Create statements that are empowering, positive, and future focused, written as though you have already achieved your goals.

Clarity and self-belief are your Lighthouse and your Anchor, giving you direction and a firm hold on your value. There is much more that I'd like to share with you, but these simple exercises are a great place to start to step into your true, abundant potential. My experience has shown me that the first steps toward active change are awareness and acceptance that there is a need for change, followed by the development of true willingness to make the change and a commitment to consistent action so that you turn your intentions into reality. I encourage you to be courageous and seek the help, guidance, or skills that you need so that you are able to tackle the challenges you face, whether it is overcoming personal adversity, taking your business to the next level, or stepping up to be the biggest, brightest, grandest version of yourself.

You're ready. It's time.

Lisa Rehurek

Lisa Rehurek is CEO and founder of MissSimplicity and creator of the SIMPLE Productivity System™. She teaches entrepreneurs how to win the time war so they can focus on key priorities to ensure success. Her passion is unraveling the over-complicated, chaotic, and unproductive entrepreneur. She spent 20 years in the corporate environment and has started 5 businesses. She has the distinct ability to systemize and operationalize while still being highly effective at the strategic level.

www.WinTheTimeWar.com

 www.facebook.com/MissSimplicity

 www.linkedin.com/in/lisarehurek

 http://pinterest.com/ManageMyTime

 http://www.youtube.com/managemytime

. . . .

Being able to make your life simple is an art that you must learn in order to succeed in business, and Lisa mastered it! I worked with Lisa on a few other occasions for other joint venture events that I created in the past. It has always been a great pleasure to work with her, so when I was looking for an expert in organization and time management, she was my first choice.

Thank you, Lisa, for accepting to play together one more time. I couldn't think of publishing this book without you in it.

{ LESSON 10 }

FIND TIME FOR SUCCESS
by Lisa Rehurek

Have you ever met someone who is so put together and poised, so in control, and wonder how they do it? How is it that they get so much done, have a hugely successful business, are always on time, and never seem frazzled? They never seem to skip a beat. They are the envy of every striving business owner. They seem to have figured out the secret formula for success within their business life and their personal life.

Successful people know what they want, and they chart the course and take action. It truly is that simple. But people get tripped up along the way because they don't know where they're going. You can't map out a plan if you don't know where you want to go. Obvious, maybe, but very few people take the time to lay out a solid plan and take focused action toward that plan. That's where business meets success.

YOUR RELATIONSHIP WITH TIME

Time is one of our most valuable assets. Aside from health, I would argue that it is the most valuable asset. It's a precious resource, yet most people use it foolishly.

We are our largest obstacles when it comes to managing how we spend our time. Some people thrive on living a chaotic life. They love the busy-ness and feel important when they showcase a never-ending stream of important tasks. Others have resigned themselves to the fact that it's always going to be a struggle. They have surrendered the will to make changes, and the mere mention of detangling the chaos is unfathomable.

Do you fit into either of these categories or maybe somewhere in between? The good news is that it really can be simple to get it under control.

UNDERSTANDING HOW TIME WORKS AGAINST YOU

Ooh, the mind can be a tricky little spinster. This is where it all begins. We let go of control, allow others to dictate our agenda, and fall into the trap of martyrdom or victimhood.

Your relationship with time lays the foundation. Get this on track, and you will have solved half of the equation. It's simple, yet difficult. You'll have to dig deep. You'll have to be honest and aware. You'll have to kick yourself in the patootie!

If you are willing, then making some key adjustments can make all the difference in the world. Let's talk about the four biggest areas of mind trickery around time.

Making excuses. Successful people do not make excuses. One of the biggest mistakes you can make as a business owner is to continually make excuses about why you can't get it together. If you have a daily fire drill that derails you, something is wrong. If you are constantly using the excuse that you're too tired, something is wrong. Get to the root of where the excuse sits, and then eliminate it. Be honest: What excuses are you making?

Playing the victim. You might assume that your situation is different, more complex, harder, or unique. Let me tell you, we all have "stuff" in our lives that keeps us from progress. We all have things that get in the way of us spending time on the important tasks. The quicker you accept your situation as being exactly what it is, where it is, for the reasons that exist, the more quickly you can move into a space of success. There are a million stories of people with all odds stacked against them, who end up excelling beyond anyone's wildest expectations. There is no room for victimhood in a business. It will thwart your growth immensely. Get rid of it!

Being reactive. It's time to move into a more proactive space. You can't successfully grow a business if you are constantly reacting. It breeds chaos, and you won't be respected at the level necessary to take your business to the top of the mountain. When you become proactive, you are choosing which action you take for the good of your company. You are choosing to own your position as leader of your company and creator of your destiny.

Putting others' agendas first. This is one of the hardest areas, particularly for women, to gain control over. We are used to putting others' first; we enjoy giving and helping other people succeed. But learning to say no is one of the most important traits a business owner can have. Learning to live day to day based on our own agenda, which is moving us toward our dream, is key. This doesn't assume selfishness, but rather it allows us to say no to the things that don't serve our dream or our mission. It also allows someone who is better suited to step into that space. We actually do a disservice when we take on things that are not aligned with our passion and our mission.

UNDERSTANDING HOW TO MAKE TIME WORK FOR YOU

Let me reveal a secret to you about time: You will never, ever get it all done. Once you fully accept this, you are on your way to winning the time war. As business owners, the to-do list will continue to grow; we will always have new ideas, and there will always be something else to do. The trick isn't getting it all done; the trick is knowing which pieces are important to your progress. Then make a plan and forge ahead.

You can either have a game plan by design or by default. I don't know about you, but I don't want anyone else in charge of my destiny. I want to own that because I'm the only one living this life. So I choose a game plan by design. Let's see how that works.

Prioritizing. Understanding what you're working toward is the number one step in staying on track with your time. When you have a clear vision of what you're working toward, it makes it easier to make decisions on which activities to spend your time on and where to allow people to divert your attention. In the exercise that follows, this is the first thing I have you do—to really understand your dream, your mission. Lay that foundation first so the rest of it has something to settle into.

Keeping focus. Let's face it: Most of us entrepreneurs have what's called "shiny ball syndrome." My favorite term for it is a "squirrel moment", as introduced in the movie Up. Entrepreneurs love to dabble in multiple activities; we delight in bouncing off the walls, and we thrive on idea generation. We are most definitely not known for focus. With that being said, focus is a must. As part of every day, you must focus on the activities that will move you closer to your mission. You don't have to let go of the squirrel moments; you just need a solid balance.

Planning. In the world of entrepreneurs, many feel that "plan" is an ugly four-letter word. It's not exciting, it's not new, and for most of us, planning is boring. Success isn't about continual excitement, and we can't eliminate dull activities altogether. Once you get the hang of planning, it will be quick and easy, and you'll have even more time for the excitement. Turn it into a habit and you'll barely even notice you're doing it.

Letting go of control. There comes a time in your business when you can no longer do everything yourself. This moment should come much sooner than it usually does. Start stepping out of your comfort zone and get some help. Let go of the need to control every single thing in your business, and let someone else do it better. Your time and attention should be spent on the things that you are best at—those that feed your passion. When you look at it that way, the list gets pretty short. In today's world, it's amazing how and where you can find help. Outsource tasks to contractors, interns, employees, and temporary help. Get creative. But stop doing it all yourself.

PUTTING IT TO WORK

This four-step exercise will lay the foundation for getting time to work in your favor.

Step 1:   What are you building for yourself? You need to know what you are working toward. For a twist on the traditional goal-setting task, create a storybook for yourself. Look into the future, 12 months from now, and visualize what you want your business to look like. Create this story as if it has already happened, as if it is one year from now and this is what your life looks like. Write it down. This is the ideal story of your life one year from today.

Step 2: Based on that 12-month story, make a list of all the projects that need to be completed, by quarter, in order to make that vision a reality.

Step 3: Within each project, make a list of tasks that need to be completed. A task is any activity that takes less than 60 minutes to complete. A series of tasks makes up a project.

Step 4: Schedule at least two focus hours each day, one in the morning and one in the afternoon, to work on these tasks. Turn off your phone, stop posting on social media, and put the squirrel in its cage. Do nothing but focused activities for that full hour. You will be amazed at how much you can get done.

The key is to keep it simple, and be flexible. This shouldn't be an over-complicated, strict process—that's why people give up. Keep it simple and keep moving forward, one baby step at a time.

Shawn Driscoll

Shawn Driscoll, the Trailblazers' coach, helps visionary entrepreneurs build distinctive, high-impact, high-income businesses. As a champion for pioneers and change makers, Shawn doesn't use a cookie-cutter approach to business building. Instead, she guides entrepreneurs to discover their unique Trailblazer Quotient (TQ) and use it to build a respected and influential business that honors their originality and purpose. Discover your TQ and pinpoint your unique profit path at **www.ShawnDriscoll.com**.

f **http://www.facebook.com/trailblazercoach**

𝕏 **https://twitter.com/shawnmdriscoll**

▶ **http://www.youtube.com/user/ShawnDriscollCoach**

in **www.linkedin.com/in/shawndriscoll/**

. . . .

Would you believe me if I were to tell you that I was once Shawn's client? Well, it is true. I even launched my first telesummit with her guidance. So of course when I wrote down the various topics I wanted to see covered in this book, I had no other name then hers to represent "trailblazing." Shawn has a real gift for bringing out what you don't know you are capable of, while nicely kicking you in the pants.

Thank you, Shawn. I'm deeply honored that you accepted my invitation; it means a lot to me. Nobody could have covered this topic as well as you.

{ LESSON 11 }

A CALL TO LEAD THE WAY
by Shawn Driscoll

. . . .

If you've ever…

> …felt misunderstood or like a misfit in business;

> …been pushed, coached, or advised to go in a direction you knew in your heart wasn't right for you;

> …questioned your own vision and wondered if you should just follow the crowd;

> …felt crazy, wrong, or even stupid for the decisions you've made that went against conventional wisdom; or

> …tried the "proven" ways to build your business and wondered why they didn't work for you…

Then I've got great news: You're not crazy. You're not a failure.

YOU ARE A TRAILBLAZER.

You see things that others don't. You believe in possibilities others haven't considered. You want business to be about more than making a quick buck. You do work that changes lives, so making a difference has to be part of the plan.

The more you try to fit in and follow the business "rule book" you've been handed, the more it's going to feel all wrong. Even worse, you're going to limit your impact and lose your way. As a trailblazer, change maker, or pioneer you can't rely on other people's maps. You have to navigate by your own sense of things. You must step up and lead the way.

Sure, you can learn some important business principles. You can find strategies that feel right and adapt them to your purpose. You can even get guidance from those who have gone before and blazed their own trails. But as long as you believe there is a "right way" to be successful in business, you will struggle.

Take me for example. When I left a successful corporate career and hung out my shingle as a coach, something strange happened. I became so fixated on being a "good coach" that I forgot all about being myself. I'd always been a change agent and corporate trailblazer—taking on game-changing projects, asking big questions, and supporting pioneering leaders who were changing the way business was done. Yet once I became a coach, I let all that questioning, challenging, and bigger thinking go. In focusing so much on mastering coaching, I stopped thinking for myself. I wrongly believed it wasn't "coach-like" to be opinionated or have an agenda, so I stopped asking questions. I stopped challenging myself and others to think differently. I held back the ideas and possibilities I could see for my clients. And I quickly lost my way.

Then people started calling me on it. In private conversations with colleagues or clients, I would quietly share my new idea for them, a new spin on an old business model concept, or a signature process I had mapped out, and I would consistently be asked one question: "Why aren't you talking and teaching about this?" After a while, it seemed ridiculous that my answer was "It's not coach-like," especially as I've spent a lifetime challenging "what is" in favor of "what's possible."

YOU MUST CLAIM YOUR DISTINCT POINT OF VIEW.

Your unique point of view is not a dirty little secret to be kept under wraps. In fact, it's the very thing the world needs most from you. Yet the tendency is to hold it back, to keep looking for a more acceptable message, refusing to believe that your distinctiveness is the most potent source of your ability to make a difference.

79

Your distinctiveness can be found in many places. It might be the way you approach serving your clients or the bigger vision behind your work that stands out. It could be that your particular story is the powerful catalyst that inspires and moves others. Perhaps you've got a unique style that speaks to your audience and feels fresh, fun, or inviting. And it's likely to be the one thing that people keep asking you for, even though you aren't quite sure it's anything special.

BUT I DON'T FEEL LIKE A TRAILBLAZER.

If you see things that others don't—new methods, new possibilities, new avenues to make a difference—then you are likely a trailblazer. If you ask questions most people can barely wrap their minds around and you know deep in your soul that answers are possible, you are a pioneer. If you want to be of influence and shape how work is done in your field—to make it more effective, meaningful, and accessible—then you are a change maker…even if you don't feel like one.

Most trailblazers are so busy doing their work and creating change that they don't think of themselves as pioneers, change agents, or innovators. Quite often, they resist or dismiss the idea entirely because the very thing that makes them unique, that inspires clients to come to them time and time again, is the very thing they resist, reject, and step over.

Here's why:

1. **"Please, not that!"**
   Sometimes when I share what I see with clients, they say "that can't be the heart of my work. No one's going to want that." There is a moment when they practically beg for the heart of their work to be anything else but that! They resist. They negotiate. They surrender to someone else's path by going to learn a new system or method instead of claiming their own. It feels safer to stay in the status quo, to follow rather than lead. But resisting your unique gifts and purpose is the sure path to stress, struggle, and stagnation.

2. **It's nothing special or unique.**

   Another common misunderstanding is that your work should be totally original, something that's never been done before. That's a nearly impossible task and a setup for failure. In reality, there is very little that hasn't been done somewhere else by someone else. Your job is to play up the distinct advantage that you offer. It's what helps creates fierce loyalty among your clients and followers. Being a trailblazer, change maker, or trendsetter doesn't require you to have brand new never-been-thought-of-before ideas or to invent an entirely new way of solving a problem or serving your clients. It just requires that you embrace and value the things that make you unique and distinctive. It asks you to speak your truth and share your unique point of view. This is your point of leadership.

3. **I can't promise that.**

   Most trailblazers are humble people, so there is often a fear of promising something you might not always be able to deliver. You might avoid making what you do too clear, too specific, or results oriented because you're concerned that not everyone you work with gets the exact same result. You want to be ethical and honest, but by being all-or-nothing, you step over the very thing that makes you and your work great. As a result, your message ends up mediocre and middle-of-the-road sounding because you're not taking a clear enough stand. You can let people know what it is you do without appearing hype-y, inauthentic, or overpromising. You can communicate your commitment to what's possible with full authenticity and confidence, but you have to be willing to stand for something first.

A CALL TO LEAD THE WAY.

In spite of your resistance and regardless of whether you choose to call yourself a trailblazer, the most important thing is that you not resist answering the call to lead in your own unique way. You do work that changes lives. To withhold that is doing everyone a disservice. It's a disservice to the clients you could help. It's a disservice to you to resist it and keep it under wraps. It's a disservice to the industry you serve and the impact you could make.

You have been called to lead the way. Will you step up and say yes? Review the following questions for exploration. Mediate on them. Journal about them. Discuss them with those you trust. These questions are meant to linger in your heart and mind for a while, so don't rush through them seeking a quick answer. Go for depth and daring. Cultivate the clarity required to lead.

1. Where in your work and life are you resisting, sidestepping, or hesitating?

2. What would be possible (for you, your clients, and the broader community you serve) if you released that resistance?

3. If you could only make one positive difference in this lifetime, what would it be?

4. In your heart of hearts, what do you believe is the purpose you are here to serve?

5. Are you ready to say a bold and committed "yes" to living and leading that purpose? If so, what is your first step?

The most important thing here is to feel a spark of excitement and possibility—to rise above the fear, doubt, and uncertainty that asks you to stay safe and to step into your own as a leader on a mission.

Aime Hutton

Aime Hutton, from Calgary, Alberta, Canada, is known to many as an inspirational speaker, facilitator, and best-selling author who speaks to women/girls of all ages to empower and inspire them to be brave, bold, and celebrate their unique self! She also educates and supports the next generation about the warning signs of dating violence, sharing her own journey as the Canadian Ambassador for the Freedom & Empowerment Teen Campaign.

www.wondergirlscamp.com
www.awakeninggodess.com

✉ **aime@wondergirlscamp.com**

ⓕ **https://www.facebook.com/CalgaryWGCAlberta**

ⓕ **https://www.facebook.com/pages/Freedom-Empowerment-Teen-Campaign**

ⓕ **https://www.facebook.com/Awakening.Goddess.YYC**

ⓧ **https://twitter.com/AwakeningGoddes**

ⓘ **http://www.linkedin.com/pub/aime-hutton/34/b4b/b76**

· ·

Let me start by saying that I am a "fan" of Aime—now it's official! She is love, joy, happiness, strength, and resilience all personified into this wonderful being. And yes, it was unthinkable for me not to have her share her voice in this anthology.

Thank you, Aime, my friend, for being so generous with your love. You are in my heart forever.

{ LESSON 12 }

DO I DARE MORE?

by Aime Hutton

· ·

So here you are, having your own business, and things are going amazingly well for you. Although perhaps you have a little bubbling feeling in your soul that there's more in you. What do you do? Do you listen to that little voice? Will you choose to stretch and dare more? There's a saying that the directions on how to get out of the box are on the outside of the box! All I can say for me is that 2013 has started out with a bang, doing things that I've never thought I could do before. It's only been a month, and I've been doing things that stretch me and get me thinking outside the box. Let me back up a second, though.

I've not always been this brave, I wasn't able to believe in myself, and I didn't think I deserved to be in the spotlight. Childhood was full of great adventures, although some of those adventures were not happy times for me. I was severely teased and bullied for six years during elementary school. I had teachers say that because of my "borderline" learning disabilities I would never write well. So I didn't stretch or let myself be seen. Until one day as an adult I started to dive into some personal development courses. I learned that, yes, I do deserve to be seen, that I can dream and do things that others have said I can't—or shouldn't—do. I also learned about the differences between the masculine and feminine, how each has its own strengths and qualities. I learned to let my feminine self out. Like many women, I thought that, to fit in, I had to be more masculine, dressing in neutral colors and going to my job and back home again.

However all that changed when I decided to stretch and dare one more time.

Have you ever done something that scares you? That really you had no experience in? This was me in the spring of 2010 after a couple of years of doing the personal growth work. I had the feeling—the spark—to dance again within me. From 2008 - 2010, I had been training with a top Latin and ballroom dance champion in a fitness class that fused together Latin dancing and Burlesque dancing. Many of my girlfriends were wondering what I was doing because they had seen such a shift in me. I had many of them come up to me and say "Aime, what are you doing? I want to learn what you're doing. Can you show me please?"

That got me thinking. Maybe I could start my own business, although I had no experience in doing so. How do I set my prices, how do I advertise, who can help me? I do not have a business degree from the university; I have a degree in sociology and women's studies! I felt like a fish out of water!

I knew that what I was going to teach would inspire women to tap into their Wonder Woman so they could shine. This is something that is needed in the world. So what did I start to do? I started telling friends that I'd be happy to show them some things. I began to inspire the women to move their bodies and give themselves the self-love they deserve. I still didn't really have clients, but I was doing something I was good at.

In January 2011, I went to an event dinner for the eWomen Network, having been introduced to the managing director at a different meeting a couple of days before. I only knew a couple of women attending and didn't know what all was about to happen, I just trusted the managing director. Everyone there was super friendly and wanted to know more about me, what I did, and how they could help me. Many of these women are now friends both in business and in my personal life. Being a part of the largest international networking organization for women in business has been amazing. It's all about lifting others as we all climb. If it wasn't for them, so many more doors and opportunities wouldn't have appeared to me. And I've chosen to step through the doors, daring more each time.

Just keep going is what is singing in my soul. I keep putting one foot in front of the other. I've been guided to do different activities to raise awareness in my business, such as by speaking at events. Am I scared and not sure what others will think me? "Do I dare do this?" pops into my head from time to time. Others believe in me before I am able believe in myself. I did it though, putting myself out there more to be seen to dance my own dance of life.

I started believing in myself even more. The confidence grew. I also began writing more on a blog site and eventually wrote a short story about a true life challenge that was published in the summer of 2012, in a collaborative book written by many who had never written before. This has sprung me forward into writing more. Do I dare write about other experiences in my life? For 2013, I'm going to be published in two, possibly three, additional collaborative books: the one you are reading now and possibly two others. I dare to stick myself in the spotlight of my own dance and be seen.

Speaking of daring to be seen, being named the Canadian Ambassador for the Freedom & Empowerment Teen Campaign has thrown me into the spotlight as a "go-to" person on dating violence. This global organization is supporting, educating, and empowering the next generation who have been through dating violence. With this new appointment, I've been doing things I've never done before, daring more and trusting the universe as I take each step, such as writing a press release and sharing my story of dating violence on video, which went global.

Letting others help me along the way has also been super important. Allowing others to guide me and mentor me and having "femtors" who've been in business have been a blessing. They give me ideas, suggestions, and sometimes even a push now and then to step out of my own box. One loves to ask questions, such as "What else is possible?" This question alone has sparked amazing things—being asked to be in this collaborative book for one. They all remind me to think big and to remember to ask questions. Another femtor gave a talk one day about books as a business. One of her suggestions of asking for sponsorship had me nervous as heck. If I asked, would people say yes? If I don't ask, the answer is no always. Guess what though? By asking friends who are in business to sponsor me for this new ambassadorship, I now have 4 sponsors—again, daring to step more into the spotlight and be seen.

Always listen to your heart, be still, and watch what can happen. Many experts speak of finding your "why." Mine hit me on the head this past summer, propelling me to dare more again. Creating another business for girls to empower them to be brave, be bold, and celebrate their unique self has stretched me as well, pulling together all the teachings that I've learned into one curriculum for empowering and inspiring the next generation. I'm daring to speak to students about some topics that they might not know who to talk to, such as bullying, friendship, and feeling worthy of oneself.

Each situation that I choose to dare and stretch outside my box has been a thrilling experience. I'm choosing to dare more and be fully in the spotlight of my own life. As I like to say: I am dancing to the beat of my own drum.

So my advice to you? Keep going! Dare to stretch and dream even bigger than you do now. Trust and know that you are worth more. Keep putting one foot in front of the other, believe in yourself, and let others help you!

LESSON FROM AIME:

Step 1: Write everything you do for your business down in a list.

Step 2: Rate each item on a scale of 1 to 10.

Step 3: If something is not a 10, make a note beside to indicate what has to happen to make it a 10.

Step 4: If it's already a 10, write how you can make it a 15.

Step 5: Write down at least 5 things you want to do in and for your business, yet perhaps you're afraid of. Stretch outside your box and think outside your box. No answer is silly; let go and give yourself permission to dream. Do they get you excited? Ask yourself what has to happen for each of these to take place—and write your answers down!

Jasmin Christensen

Jasmin Christensen, PhD Counseling Psychology, is the founder of Healing Connections and Pathways. She has nothing less than 20 years of counseling and teaching experience to share with the world. Among all her talents, she is also a national and international lecturer. Jasmin is an experienced on-site trauma and disaster counselor (e.g., 9/11 in New York City). Her unique connections with people, on a general basis, make her a popular and empathic counselor and life coach. Being a multiple sclerosis patient herself, Jasmin has the firsthand experience of overcoming almost insurmountable odds just to achieve daily tasks.

www.healingconnectionsandpathways.com

www.facebook.com/Healingconncections

https://twitter.com/Greeneyedgoddes

Jasmin is my "life savior," so to speak. Whenever I think "I can't," she is just one DM away. She is just unbelievable. I cannot find the words to describe how profoundly she has impacted my life and my business. She is the living proof that "impossible" is just an invention of the mind. She is an extraordinary woman.

Thank you, Jasmin, from the bottom of my heart for allowing me to showcase your beauty in this book.

GETTING OUT OF YOUR OWN WAY

by Jasmin Christensen, PhD Counseling Psychology

Ah yes, you find yourself faced with the impossible challenge of having a chronic illness. You've struggled along, finally to be told what particular monster will be your lifelong companion now. Mine is multiple sclerosis, and it reared its ugly head into my life about 15 years ago. What do you do when your life is no longer what you knew it to be? How does a physically fit and very active person cope with the day-to-day challenges of such an illness? Heck, how do you move past this to even think about having a career or a business or any of our dreams that we held so dear? It's not easy, but it is possible. Read on, this story does get better.

I was the kind of person who was always very active and physically fit. I had been a US Marine in my 20s and believed in keeping an active lifestyle. I swam a mile a day, played adult league softball with my husband, trained several days a week with my German Shepherd pup, and kept up with my teenage boys and all of their school and after-school activities. I also worked at a job I loved and did my bit as a corporate wife with the odd corporate function. My life was good, and I never gave any of it a second thought. I knew where I was headed and how I was going to get there. Then, out of the blue, the universe back-handed me—or at least that's how it felt. My life fell apart as quickly as my body did.

As the illness slowly took hold of my life and the ugly diagnosis of multiple sclerosis (MS) was delivered to me, with instructions to simply go home and make the best of things, I railed against what fate had handed me. I didn't want to simply "go home and make the best of things." I wanted to work, to compete, to attend my sons' football games. I wanted my life back! That wasn't going to happen any time soon—in fact, not at all. My old life was gone, and any prospects of working or having a career were pretty much out the window. So what to do next? That was the real question.

There I was, on my sofa, angry at the world. I was also angry at my own body for having betrayed me. I couldn't wrap my head around the fact that someone who had always been so athletic and physically fit could now not even trust her own feet to carry her across the floor. I wasn't able to manage a full day of activities anymore. Simply going to the grocery store was a challenge. Oh yes, I was in a full-blown "pity party" with all the trimmings, whining, complaining, and talking about what I used to do, the life I used to have, as well as the occasional snot-slinging wailing meltdowns. No, it wasn't a pretty sight, but it was part of the process. Part of the lovely privilege of having MS is that you have flare-ups; when you get back on your feet, you have another flare-up down the road. You get better, but never 100%; you are always aware of what bit of yourself has been compromised, what part of you hasn't come back. What did I do to work past all of that and get to where I am now? Well, it wasn't some magical fairy godmother with her wand or anything like that. Oh no, nothing that easy.

I got better, and I didn't think about MS again until a few years later when it reared up again and smacked me right between the eyes. This flare-up was much worse than the earlier bout. This is when the real fear set in. All of the emotional stuff that I had swept under the rug had to be faced this time. I couldn't just pretend that it didn't exist. I was barely able to crawl to the toilet on bad days, so I had to face up to what was right in front of me: The 400-pound monster that was not only in the room, but was also hitching a ride on my shoulders demanded to be acknowledged. I was stuck on the sofa again (yeah, it's a familiar theme) and in the middle of rural USA. The acreage we lived on was beautiful, wild, and very isolated. Town was a good 30-minute drive down the mountain. I was literally stuck with no one around and nowhere to go. My husband would come home, look at me on the sofa, and go into the bedroom and close the door. He didn't know how to deal with me either. If it hadn't been for my sons coming by to check on me, I would probably have died of starvation and thirst.

Finally, I had to face it all. I was in bed, a rare occasion, and had to go to the toilet. My legs were not cooperating. I had a choice to make: either piss myself and be forced to lay in it until my husband got home or drag myself into my bathroom and handle it myself. I chose the latter. It took me minutes of dragging myself out of bed, on the wrong side no less to be closer to the bathroom, and pulling myself up on the furniture, door jambs, walls, and counters, but by God I made it with bare seconds to spare. I sat on that toilet for long moments past what I needed to. I sat there and had to make the decision to get back up. By the time I reached the stool in front of my dressing counter, I was covered in sweat and red faced, but that day was a turning point for me. I refused to let this thing stop me, confine me, hamper me, or turn me into a person who couldn't live my life. The oddest phrase was repeating through my brain—a phrase one of my old Master Sergeants used to tell us when we had insurmountable odds back in the Corps. I could hear his old raspy voice yelling in my head, "Well come on, ladies, use your brains—there's more than one way to skin a freakin' cat." Yeah, weird, I know, but it's what was reverberating through my brain. In regular person speak, that meant that it was time to think outside of the box.

From that day on I learned that I had to focus—sometimes extremely hard and with laser sharpness—to move forward, hell, even just to move on some days. I knew I wasn't destined to spend my time on the sofa, so I finished up my advanced degrees online and did my clinicals at facilities that understood my illness and were willing to work with me. Through it all, my area of expertise began to get clearer and my path was set. I was bound and determined to run my own business and do what I loved: counseling. I even set up a second phone line in the house so that if I was having a bad flare-up and couldn't drive I could still attend to clients from the house. That was how my business Healing Connections and Pathways was born.

So, what would I recommend for others in this or a similar spot? Do a daily practice that I still do to this day: Before I even get out of bed, I focus on all the things that I am grateful for. It's like a mind-clearing exercise that grounds me into what is real and what is not. Then I spend a few moments focusing on what my goal is, whether it's a small one or a larger project goal. Through this practice, I can visualize like crazy and have found it to be a very valuable tool. Spend a week starting each day looking at what you are grateful for—it really does work at re-centering yourself. Then focus—I mean really focus—and visualize what your goal is. You will find that doing this daily, even for only a week, will make a huge difference. Does this work, you ask? Yes, if focusing so intensely that I can make MS-damaged nerves in my legs work, then that same focus can achieve business goals, life goals, and just about anything. The real key is to not stop, not give up. After all, what have you got to lose?

Toni Coleman Brown

Toni Coleman Brown is an author, coach, and motivational speaker. She is also the CEO and founder of the Network for Women in Business, an online community for women business owners who seek affordable cutting-edge training and the ability to connect and advance with other like-minded individuals. Toni lives in Queens, New York, with her husband and two daughters.

www.networkforwomeninbusiness.com

 toni@networkforwomeninbusiness.com

. . . .

I first met Toni last year during a training call I did for her network. From the first minute to the last, I was in awe. Toni was nothing but calmness, confidence, and strength. I kept asking myself "How did she manage to build an empire on Facebook in just 11 months (at the time) and be so calm?" I know social media remains a big black hole for many women out there, which is why I really wanted this subject to be covered and I only wanted Toni to do it. What she has been capable of achieving through Facebook and in just a short period of time is nothing less than really inspiring.

Thank you, Toni, for walking alongside with me once again. You are a Facebook queen!

{ LESSON 14 }

30 DAYS TO FACEBOOK MASTERY
by Toni Coleman Brown

. . . .

Okay, so if you haven't already noticed this, I'm here to tell you that social media is here to stay. Businessmen and -women all over the world are desperately trying to "master" it, and they're paying big money to social media strategists to help them dominate their niche— all with the hopes of driving traffic and paying customers to their websites. But is it mandatory to be a multi-million dollar company to build a strong following of engaged fans?

Absolutely not!

A few months ago, I received a call from the corporate offices of Facebook. They told me that I had one of the most active fan pages on Facebook and wanted to help me grow more fans, of course for a large fee. I almost flipped my wig! I couldn't believe that little ole' me, a 47-year-old mom, wife, and fun-loving entrepreneur had cracked the code and built a bulging fan base that's been growing virally every day. I was stunned that I had done something that only 6% of fan page owners had ever done.

Well, like Oprah often says, "here is what I know for sure…." If I could do it, then so can you. With the information I share in this chapter, you too can master Facebook in 30 days.

Day 1:   Create a strategy. Ask yourself who it is that you're trying to target. Is it men or women? How old are they? What do they like? Where do they live? Knowing this type of information ahead of time is vital to your success because Facebook's unique platform allows you to target your marketing efforts to these types of specific demographics.

Day 2:   Create your fan page and make sure to use a custom URL that is the same as your website. For example, our home site is **http://www.networkforwomeninbusiness. com** and our FB fan page URL is **www.facebook.com/ networkforwomeninbusiness**. If you don't know how to do this, simply go to the help section of Facebook and search for "custom URL."

Day 3:   Create a timeline cover and custom tabs that are consistent with your website design. It's important that your brand image be consistent with your website so your visitors are not confused. Hire someone to do this for you if you want it to look professional.

Day 4:   Link your website to your fan page by adding social media icons that link directly to your fan page. Make sure that your home website is prominently positioned in the "About" section of your Facebook fan page directly under your profile picture.

Day 5:   Make sure that a least one of your custom tabs provides a link from your fan page to your home website. Better yet, find an app or company like Heyo.com that will allow you to drop your website directly into one of your tabs on Facebook so your visitors don't have to leave Facebook to browse your website.

Day 6:   Start getting fans. Begin with who you know by sending an email to everyone in your contact list and all of your current Facebook friends. Don't expect them all to oblige and don't take it personally if they don't.

Day 7:   Get more fans by contacting some of your friends who might have a large friend base and ask them to promote your new fan page to their friends.

Day 8:   Create an engagement ad to get new "likes." An engagement ad is one that encourages action. For example, you can say, "Click LIKE if you want to lose weight this year." This would be a great engagement ad for a fan page dedicated to weight loss.

Day 9:   Get more followers by trying a site like Fiverr.com, but be careful because some of the people who claim to have hundreds of thousands of followers might be promoting some unsavory things, and you don't want those types of people as a part of your fan base.

Day 10:   If you haven't already done so, make sure to add your fan page to your email signature. This will ensure that everyone you come in contact with is aware of your fan page.

Day 11:   Develop a content strategy. Your content should in most cases (but certainly not all cases) drive people to your website. Content includes blog posts, videos, articles, etc.

Day 12:   Use lots of pictures as a part of your content. Facebook users love photos, and they like to share them. Find them and post them on your fan page. These types of posts always go viral, and they always bring in new likes for free!

Day 13:   Stay relevant and active. Make sure that you never abandon your fans. They will begin to depend on you to keep feeding them with information.

Day 14:   Subscribe to RSS feeds from websites and blogs that have information that your community would find interesting and use this information on your page.

Day 15:   Make sure to use calls to action (CTAs), such as "Click LIKE if...." Facebook users like to be told what to do.

Day 16:   Make sure that you use social share and connect buttons to share your blog posts on your fan pages. Your blogs will always contain valuable content that you won't want your fans to miss.

Day 17:   Take your fans off of your Facebook fan page and get them on your list as fast as possible. Do this by telling them to join your mailing list. Tell them this often.

Day 18:   Make sure to use Page Post Promotions often because the truth is that most of the people who like your page will never return to it. Page Post Promotion is a great way to make sure that your page/posts are being viewed.

Day 19:   Learn to make Facebook Insights your friend. Use it to analyze your statistics. Check it to see what types of posts have given you the most engagement. Use it to see which ones went more viral. Find out where your fans reside. What's their age? Do you have more female fans or male? This type of information is priceless when growing a business using social media.

Day 20:   Once you figure out what works, continue to do more of those actions. You might even want to double up on those actions. If you keep giving people more of what they like, they will keep looking for you. This way your fans will become super fans.

Day 21:   When you find out what doesn't work, stop doing it immediately. There is no need to waste your time or money.

Day 22:   Develop a monthly content calendar based on strategies and posts that work—namely, what went viral, got you new likes, got your community talking, etc.

Day 23:   Super fans will suddenly appear. They're the ones always making comments and always sharing info. You might want to consider giving one of them administrative rights so they can help you build your community. And they will probably say yes and do it for free because they're super fans and will volunteer to help you.

Day 24:   Once you begin to build an active community, begin to think about social media dominance and encourage your fans to follow you on your other social media platforms, such as Twitter, LinkedIn, Google+, and more.

Day 25:   Stay on top of the changes. Facebook's new Edgerank algorithm makes it harder to get your information in front of your entire fan base, which is why Page Posts Promotions are a must. They're reasonable, which is why you should use them as much as possible.

Day 26:   Utilize contests and other fan involvement activities to keep things moving and fresh. For example, you can say something like: Fill in the blank. One word to describe my business is _____.

Day 27:   Keep it fun. Create contests and other fan involvement activities to keep it exciting.

Day 28:   The next time you host a live teleseminar or webinar, instead of having Q&A over the phone or on your webinar chat box, use your fan page for the chatting. This will ensure engagement on your fan page.

Day 29:   Make sure you always use shareable content on your page post, like videos and pictures. Simple text posts—although they can promote engagement—are not shareable. This means that these posts will never go viral.

Day 30:   Rinse and repeat: Once you figured out what's working for your niche and your fans keep doing those actions over and over again month after month, don't stop and don't ever give up.

Monique Alamedine

Monique's "aha" moment happened at a marketing seminar, when she realized that she was hiding behind her product! As spectacular as her bodysuits were, she was using them as an excuse to play small. As the Business Blingstress, Monique's mission is to empower heart-centered women to play big, monetize their strengths, and command success in their life + business. She is building a business empire, which includes the revolutionary Snugbods Bodysuits and the eco-stylish Glass Straws.

www.moniquealamedine.com
www.GlassStraws.com.au
www.Snugbods.com.au

✉ monique@snugbods.com
f www.facebook.com/BusinessBlingstress
f www.facebook.com/GlassStraws
f www.facebook.com/Snugbods
🐦 www.twitter.com/moniquealam
🐦 www.twitter.com/glassstraws
🐦 www.twitter.com/snugbods
📌 www.pinterest.com/moniquealam

• •

Monique is one of the numerous people I met through this project. She breathes experience and give it back tenfold to her audience. I have no doubt you'll enjoy her chapter and that you'll learn valuable information.

Thank you, Monique, for accepting the challenge and helping this book shine in the world.

LIVING LIFE UNFULFILLED
by Monique Alamedine

· ·

Lost, tired, unmotivated, unworthy, empty—these are the words that describe how it felt being dictated to at work, clocking in and out. Ten years into my recruitment career and I was just about existing and maintaining a façade, getting sick at the thought of going to work. While the monotonous office politics went on around me, I was hating life, getting sick, and becoming an emotional wreck. I was not only detached and disconnected from myself, but from everyone. Disorganization ruled my house and home. I had no time with my family, and fun was a distant notion.

My journey started here in this desperation, knowing there had to be more out there for me. Intuitively, I felt strongly that I could live a dream life, but it didn't lie here in my corporate job; the money was great, but there was no depth, and everything was power suits, high heels, and full makeup.

Corporate just wasn't doing it for me internally anymore.

SAME CHARADE, DIFFERENT FAÇADE

When I stumbled across life coaching, the spiritual door was already opening for me. I'd started a journey of discovery, going within and doing healing work when I found Louise Hay and Doreen Virtue, then went on to become an angel intuitive. When I heard the term "life coach," I didn't even know what it was, but something inside of me knew that's what I needed to be, so I got busy studying.

The first client that walked in the door was a $20,000 corporate client. Nothing had changed!

COMPILED BY **CHRISTINE MARMOY**

It still didn't resonate with me. It didn't feel right. I still had this whole "got-it-together" image. I still wore suits. I was still dealing with the corporate world. I still knew this was not my dream.

When I became pregnant, it was a bittersweet time. I'd just started my business, but I stopped work anyway because I just couldn't function with baby brain. Luckily for me, I had my baby girl and things changed again. I started yet another business. Snugbods Bodysuits was created out of a need for bodysuits to make women feel sleek and look chic—and for me to stop wearing three tops at a time, post-pregnancy! I started the business all well and good. I had great media coverage. Then it all stopped. It didn't feel right. It wasn't perfect.

THE BUSINESS DISCONNECT

Have you always wanted to know the secret of how other entrepreneurs shine in their businesses? I wondered what I was doing wrong. I felt like an imposter. I didn't feel I was being real. I didn't have depth.

The mistake I made when starting my life-coaching business was setting up all of the external elements first: the website, the offerings, all those things you think you need to make a business a business. Yet there was a disconnect between what was happening externally in my business and internally within myself. Somewhere, my beliefs and values had separated from what I was doing. There was me as my business persona and then there was the spiritual me.

When this happens, you feel as if you are living a double life. You are constantly chasing your tail, feeling like a fraud. There is no peace. Inside, you know there's got to be more to running your business than what's happening now. You want to make more money. You're tired of having two personalities. You want to show more "you" in the business.

THEY WANT TO BUY THE STORY

Nothing happened with Snugbods Bodysuits for a year. One day, my husband asked me what I was afraid of, and it dawned on me. I was afraid of success because it meant putting myself out there.

So I re-launched, without waiting for everything to be perfect. It felt better and less inhibited, but still not there. As time went on, I was able to share more of myself and get more real, but it wasn't until I went to a marketing seminar on my own that I noticed how small I'd been playing. I'd been hiding behind my product until I learned this one simple lesson that has since become my life mission to teach:

Nobody wants to buy a product; they want to buy the story.

People want to buy what you are selling as a person. It's about marrying your deep values with your business structure so that everything is aligned.

IT'S ABOUT AUTHENTICITY

Learning to be authentic was a massive turning point for me. Suddenly, I felt guided to do this work with other women. Intuitively, I felt strongly that this was how I could live a dream life. Why? Because creating a business with all that external stuff means nothing without a strong sense of self. Because I feel with every part of my being that we are moving into a new era where authenticity matters. We no longer live in the fake world we knew before. We want transparency. We want authenticity. People are picking up on what's right and what's not. You can't hide any more. We are all human; we all connect.

Connection is the very core of business. Business is an exchange of energy. Even if two people have the same product, people might resonate more with one business owner than another because of the connection. For your people to connect with you, you need to share yourself.

For your business to connect and shine, you have to resonate with the people you are teaching and they will be drawn to you. They will feel your authenticity. They will feel the connection because you are living and breathing it.

HOW DO I GET AUTHENTIC?

Being authentic is a journey, and it isn't easy. I get it! In practical terms, it really can be step by step, but it has to start with you.

1. It's about taking stock of who you are. It's about reflecting, going within, journaling, meditating, finding a mentor who knows what it's like to walk in your shoes, and talking to people who have been there before.

Ask yourself:

- What do I stand for?

- What am I against?

- What legacy do I want to leave behind?

- How am I nourishing my mind, body, and spirit daily?

- Where am I allowing fear to creep in?

2. Then it's about stopping. Authenticity is an inward journey. I was constantly go, go, go, flying by the seat of my pants. This made my business reactive rather than proactive. Being reactive is a lack of self-love, a sabotage technique, maintaining fight-or-flight mode, rather than laying down a structure for your business to grow and evolve. Instead, it is about having a business foundation and balancing that with the authentic, spiritual you.

- Get balance and structure for your life and business:

- Think about what is in the food you eat (sugar, dairy, wheat).

- Find what you enjoy in your business.

- Find what is important in your business.

- Where the two do not match, consider outsourcing.

- Create rituals for yourself as much as you systemize your business.

3. Authenticity is simplicity. Are you the kind of person who has to cook with 10 ingredients to feel like you're making something taste good? One day, I saw this simple cashew recipe with 2 ingredients. For some reason, the penny dropped. I used to feel like I had to add so many things to make something great. I would have put in maybe 7 or so ingredients because I felt that was what it needed. This simple, 2-ingredient recipe that I loved was a catalyst for another shift in my life. I always remind myself of that. When I look at cashews now, I think of simplicity. They are an analogy for living a simpler life.

4. Last of all, start living it!

The Authentic You

In short, authenticity sells. If you align your personal brand, you can bring in the bling in your business—there's no doubt about it. I can say without hesitation that introducing structure to your intuitive sense of self creates a brand that you can not only enjoy, but that will also earn you more.

Marrying the two together has made me feel stronger. We all need to keep working on our fears of putting ourselves out there. The real you is who people want to see.

For my part, I'm a work in progress. Sometimes I still feel very raw and bare, but there is something inside of me that intuitively knows that this is where I need to be. It feels different from my business before. Now my business feels right and resonates. I used to think it was so hard, but I feel good even on bad days now because I trust that it's all falling into place. You can't put a price on that feeling of certainty, that inner knowing.

Business and life become all-encompassing: Family life, health, wholeness, and wellness meld into one when you live and do business as your authentic self. This business approach has turned things around. Mentors have noticed a difference in me. Even my husband has noticed!

I love bringing together all aspects of my life like this—my love of rap music, dancing, spirituality, alkalizing green foods—and just inserting the structure to make it a business. As I always say:

Intuition + Structure = Business Bling!

Kim Boudreau Smith

Kim Boudreau Smith, CEO of Kim Boudreau Smith Inc., creator of PowerUp Inside/Out, mentoring women who are STRENGHTENING the World!; Inspirational speaker and Author. Kim proves to be a direct, no-nonsense cheerleader for her clients, taking them to "strengthening their inner foundation-building core muscle" in their business and life to becoming clear on their direction and powering-up to the next level. Kim excelled in corporate America and owned a fitness company; supporting hundreds of women obtain healthier lifestyles inside and out.

www.kimboudreausmith.com

. . . .

Kim is another gem who was given to me through a friend. Although I have never met Kim personally—face to face, that is—I had the immense pleasure to spend a couple of hours with her over Skype. She also holds a big "why" and wears it on her sleeves. She is a true people person, and I'm sure you'll drink in her words, just the way I did it.

Thank you, Kim, for the delightful conversation we had and for being so supportive of this project.

{ LESSON 16 }

HOME IS WHERE THE HEART IS...
by Kim Boudreau Smith

· ·

Didn't Dorothy click her heels and say "there is no place like home?" Right before this, Glenda the Good Witch told her that the answer to finding her way back home has been inside of her all along. How come we still tend to look for joy, happiness, love, decisions, and so much more, including success, outside of us? To become crystal clear on our purpose takes answers from within. This is living on our own terms, joyously, authentically, prosperously, and successfully! How do we get there and do we ever fully arrive? Where to begin?

To begin is awareness.

STEP ONE

Becoming aware—achieving consciousness, wakefulness, mindfulness—leads to understanding that the current mindset, feeling, and lifestyle are not where you would like to be, that you desire change, but do not know where to begin. Awareness is the first step. This begins by awakening the inner wisdom we all have. When we live in our heads, we live by others' standards, judgments of ourselves, traditions, and expectations that are not our own, which keep us further from our truth and our true being. Staying in our heads keeps us as human doers, not beings. This is a far distant quantum leap from our heart. So become aware of what the struggles, pain, and resistance are in your life. It took me falling asleep behind the steering wheel of my car at a major intersection in the middle of a beautiful, bright sunny day—not once, but twice—to realize that my business and my life was dead asleep. I was living without passion; I was burnt out and beaten down, all by me! No, I didn't hurt anyone or myself that day, but—no pun intended—what a wakeup call! I instantly became aware that I was not living my true me, my passionate calling. I was sick and tired of being tired. I had a real story going on in my head. I couldn't even feel my heart beating, let alone listen to my heart whispering. Success is in the heart; the true knowing is there as well.

Dorothy kept following a yellow brick road that was leading to…? I am sure in her mind she thought that answers were in the Wicked Witch's broom being brought back to the Wizard, who would show Dorothy the way home. The Wizard was just another man who really didn't have the answers for her. This kept Dorothy away from the power-filled truth that is within. I find it very interesting that she could gather up a community of others to follow the yellow brick road with her also in search of a heart, courage, and a brain.

STEP TWO

Discovering our self-success involves gathering up a community: a coach, a mentor, friends—people who can support us and keep us accountable. There are many programs that can support women who have this desire, but are unclear of where to turn to next. We are unable to do this alone, and we are not designed to be alone, so create your community, tribe, or circle of support. Don't waste another moment. The world is waiting for you—you are waiting for you!

STEP THREE

Recognize that we have an inner critic, better known as the bitch in the attic, and she keeps us from our personal and professional successes. She is really good at this because she has been running the show your whole life. Think of her like this: Do you have children? Remember when they were young and you would get on the telephone—what did they do? Possibly begin crying, whining, or chant "mommy, mommy, mommy," perhaps tugging on your pant leg for attention, right? Either you ignored them or you said to them "hush I'm on the phone," and then what did they do? They either got louder or they went to another room to find some trouble. Those little kids grew up to be teenagers and became louder and stronger, right? The same thing happens with our inner critic/ego/bitch in the attic. She grows up, becomes stronger, and—when you decide to do something different and make changes to your life—she begins her upheaval of a personality. Then she begins her chanting: "You can't do that or this; you will never amount to anything, so don't even try; you're not good enough and who do you think you are?" When her noise-filled voice doesn't work, she brings in anxiety and depression, to name a few, to keep you in the same place. (This is our personal tantrum.) She believes you don't know what you are doing, not to mention being, and all it takes is to let her know that you can manage your life now and thank her for being there for you. We need her, but on our terms, not hers. To begin to manage her (not control, manage), claim your true "I am" affirmation statements. This will support your inner critic through these changes. Examples of I am statements:

- I am confident.

- I am a passionate, grateful, and loving being.

- I am successful.

- I am a power-filled audacious woman.

Do not hold back. This might feel strange at first; usually doing something different from our comfortable usual way feels different or "off" at first. Put these "I am" statements on Post-it notes and post them on your mirror, in your car, on your desk—keep them in sight. The most famous speakers, coaches, and authors practice this to manage nerves and limiting beliefs and to continue to grow personally and professionally. Do not give up. Gather up your community and let them know what you are doing to become your successful self; ask them to support you and hold you accountable. We cannot do this alone. If you think you can, your critic is still doing the talking!

STEP FOUR

The last step, but definitely not the least, is taking care of you. I refer to this as "bubble bath" moments. Remember the Calgon commercial? "Calgon, take me away!" Take the time to nurture yourself and care for you. We schedule everyone and everything else on our calendars, yet we overlook scheduling time for us. We say "someday…." Well, someday is not a day! Here are some suggestions for self-caring:

- Draw a bubble bath

- Slow down in the middle of the day and take some deep breaths

- Go for a walk

- Practice yoga

- Read a mindless novel

- Meditate

- Schedule a "hooky day" and do a few things you wouldn't do: coffee and a croissant at a local bakery, a matinee movie, window shop, and day dream

- Take up a hobby: art, dancing, or poetry writing

As children we used our imagination all the time, as adults we very rarely let ourselves go into our imaginations. Take it away—anything is possible!

1. I would like to leave you with a few more questions to consider:

2. What do you want your life to feel and look like?

3. What do you solve?

4. What do you love to do that will lead you to your "being" and your passion?

Go to the end of this year and look back: What does this past year look and feel like?

Remember, don't hold back, and manage the bitch in the attic. Your passionate true you is right there, waiting to be!

All it takes is awareness, desire, willingness, a moment to slow down and feel your heart, deep breaths (a lot of those), "I am" positive affirmation statements, and really taking care of you! This is the mixture for self-success. Don't beat yourself up when you make mistakes; there will be times for mistakes, as we are only human. Embrace yourself daily and acknowledge yourself with positive and warm love!

This is how we build muscle and strength from the inside out! Home is where the heart is, it is a muscle and it needs to be strengthened, DAILY!

Catrice M. Jackson

Catrice M. Jackson, Speaker, *BOSSLady of Branding* and Irresistible Personal Branding Expert helps women business owners create an irresistible personal brand in 30 days, speak on stage with authentic confidence and create brand messaging that attracts clients they crave. Catrice is a two time international best-selling author and the author of three self-help inspirational books, has been in the Law of Attraction Magazine and received the 2012 Stiletto Women in Business Award for Entrepreneur of the Year in Education and Training for inspiring and empowering women world-wide. *Catriceology*, her signature coaching secret-sauce, anchored in truth, authenticity and freedom, is what Catrice uses to empower womenpreneurs to release the soul of their personal brand for business success on their own terms.

www.catriceology.com

✉ **Email: catriceology@gmail.com**

𝐟 **Facebook: www.facebook.com/bossladybrands**

🐦 **Twitter: www.twitter.com/catriceology**

▶ **Catriceology TV: www.youtube.com/catriceology1**

Radio: www.blogtalkradio.com/catriceology

· ·

Catrice is a heartfelt friend. I'm honored to count her among the stars included in this book. She is a voice, she is a persona, she is love. She has a way with words, and she knows how to help you tap into the brilliance you don't even always realize you have.

Thank you, Catrice, for being one of my best "virtual" friends. You know this book couldn't go to print without you in it.

{ LESSON 17 }

STRUT YOUR WAY TO SUCCESS WITH A THOUGHT-LEADER BRAND

by Catrice M. Jackson

Do you really understand and know the power within you? I'm not talking about a physical or mental strength that can be calibrated and measured. I'm referring to an invisible, invincible essence within you that can never be duplicated or stolen. It's deeply and beautifully woven into your divine DNA, whether you want it to be or not. This overwhelming power is simply defined as the power and brand of you. No matter what you do in the world you *are* a brand. As a business owner, you are the face of the brand, so anchor deeply into that powerful essence and use it as the soul-source of your success.

There's an old branding mindset that many people still believe and utilize in their business. Let's look at the brand of you from that old branding perspective. A few things that create business success are having a fantastic product for sale, a clear and effective sales strategy, and marketing and advertising that showcase the value and benefits of your product as well as knowing who your target market and clients are, to name just a few. If you are running your business using the outdated branding mindset, you'll only see the importance of a brand when it's time to add your product to the website and sell it.

However, if you've adopted a *thought-leader* branding mindset, you know for certain that you cannot effectively do any of the above without first considering how that product is birthed from, expands, and strengthens your brand. If you're not always starting with your brand, when you create new products, develop other services, or market your business, you are sabotaging your success. Thought leaders know that a brand is the most valuable asset of their business, yet many business owners invest very little time, money, energy, or effort into creating, cultivating, and managing it. Your brand holds equal power to that of your physical heart. Once your heart stops beating, you die. If your brand has no life or pulse, your business dies as well. Today's the day you think of your brand this way. It is critical that you invest in your brand as it's the single most essential thing you can do with your time, money, and energy if you want to experience the success you envision and serve with greater impact.

A thought-leading mindset of branding you and your business requires you to discover that power within, release its brilliance, own the expert authority of that power, communicate it with influence, and leverage every single ounce of it in your life, relationships, and business. A thought-leading brand is distinctively recognized as the go-to expert brand of choice within a certain industry. Thought-leading brands earn and maximize this distinction, thereby commanding and defending higher rates for their products—and people pay them. Consider *BMW*, *Versace*, *Tiffany*, *Apple*, or even *Kellogg*; we don't question the quality, we just buy the brand because they've proven their brand is worth it, period.

Thought-leading brands innately create other lucrative benefits, such as global impact, market influence, brand ambassadors, and social legacy. When you unapologetically and boldly communicate the brilliance within, you can use your brand to champion causes and people will join you. You make more money because your brand's equity is resilient in any economy. A thought-leading brand works for you instead of you working hard to make money. A thought-leading brand easily magnetizes brand ambassadors who eagerly praise and promote your genius, thereby expanding your impact and influence. When your brand is able to do all of this, you make your mark in the world marketplace and leave a brand legacy that thrives when you are no longer here.

You might not desire a brand as big as *Apple* or *BMW*, but consider branding as big as you desire within your industry to leverage your brand's uniqueness and strengthen your brand equity. Creating and cultivating a strong brand allows you to work less and enjoy life more by reducing the hours you spend hustling up clients. If you brand "right" and let your brand work for you, you'll have clients chasing you; then all you've got to do is say yes.

Here are ten of my best strategies for becoming a thought-leading brand:

1. Relentlessly believe that you are the brand—all the time, everywhere, and with everyone. Thought leaders know they're a brand and don't have reservations about stepping up, blazing an innovative trail, and creating a new trend that makes their mark in the marketplace.

2. Stop cutting corners and taking the cheap route to build your brand. Your brand is your number one business asset. Without a clear, relevant, and distinctive brand, you risk being invisible in the marketplace. Invest the money, time, and energy into branding "right" and let your brand work for you while you live, love, and play.

3. Become your own brand expert. Don't make the mistake of just letting someone else create a brand for you; co-create it and learn everything you can about brand marketing success. Empower your business by staying on top of the greatest brand development strategies. Don't be afraid to re-invent, refresh, rebuild, or revitalize your brand; be your brand's expert.

4. Be you, be real. Potential clients are craving deeper, more personal and authentic relationships and experiences with business owners. Never compromise, hide, or diminish your unique brilliance. In fact, turn up the volume by stripping away all the social expectations and let the world see the real, authentic you.

5. Stop hiding. Your business can't afford for you to hide who you are anymore. You were uniquely created, so move your ego out of the way and reveal the real you with confidence! Your business is a service, and it's not about you, it's about serving the world. Maximize the power of your brand by deeply anchoring into the fact that there's no one with your talent, wisdom, experience, and genius. Step up as an expert and shine!

6. Brand from the inside out. The most irresistible and visible brands are those that exude a clear and pulsating "why." People buy your why—the passion, purpose, vision, and core essence of why you do what you do and why you offer the products you do. What's your deep soulful why? Communicate it to your ideal clients, live it, be it, show up, and exude your why so they can feel it.

7. Release your Irresistible Trademark (IT). Market your brilliance like a millionaire. Millionaires are not afraid to market their genius; that's how they made their millions. What is the most irresistible thing about you? What's that thing you do better than others in your industry? It's there; look deep, and when you find it you'll discover your Irresistible Trademark. Put the stamp of you into everything you do by showcasing your juicy spot of genius and marketing it with meaning and memorable magnetism.

8. Master your craft and cash in. Become a recognized expert within your niche. Consistently do research within your industry to stay on the cutting edge to keep your brand relevant and distinctive. Don't be afraid to walk on the wild side and release your creative juices. Business owners who are standing out, shining, and succeeding are those who have embraced thought-leader branding by letting the real, creative, fully expressed woman out to play. If you want your brand to make money, use this *Catriceology* formula: Confidence + Courage = Cash.

9. Create a robust online brand presence. Put some vavoom into your brand visibility. Blah, blah, blah brand marketing is so vanilla. Your ideal clients crave more from your marketing messages. They want a 3-D expression of who you are, what you believe in, and what you stand for; they want to feel your soul. Excite, ignite, inspire, intrigue, and captivate them with luscious on-brand language that speaks directly to what they need, want, value, and expect in order to communicate that you are the solution to their problem.

10. Step onto the platform and shine. Seize every opportunity to speak about your ideas, products, and programs with passion. Master the art of storytelling by showing potential clients what working with you feels like instead of telling them. Bring your brand to life in video

117

by creating videos that inform, educate, inspire, and motivate people into action. Host your own radio show, be a guest speaker, and share the power of your brand on every platform possible.

Your brand is the most valuable asset of you and your business. Invest in it and let it work for you. When your brand is "right," it can never be duplicated. Celebrate and showcase your **you**niqueness and live your big dreams. Your dreams are made for walking, so don't just talk about them, be about them. Break away from the pack, step into your soulful, sassy self, and strut your way to success by being a thought-leading brand, taking it all the way to the bank.

Cha-ching

…see you at the top, leading lady!

Nancy Meadows

Nancy Meadows has been an interior designer since 2002. After years spent in the beauty and fashion industries, she transitioned to owning her own award-winning day spa before transitioning once again to study interior design, a life-long passion. She works with heart-centered women who appreciate the psychological importance of having a home that is not only functional and beautiful, but also excites all of their senses and allows them to live their very best lives. Her favorite quote is from Coco Chanel: "It's not the rooms; it's the life you live in them."

www.NancyMeadowsDesigns.com

✉ **me@nancymeadowsdesigns.com**

f **http://www.facebook.com/NancyMeadowsInteriorDesign**

🐦 **https://twitter.com/Nancy Meadows**

in **http://www.linkedin.com/in/nancymeadowsinteriordesign**

I met Nancy through a Mastermind group we both belong to and what I noticed right away was her voice. She has a beautiful voice, one that you could hear telling you bedtime stories; it is a reassuring voice, a grounded voice, and a powerful yet soft voice. Her approach to interior design was so compelling that I felt the urge to invite her to participate in this project, and I'm really blessed that she said yes.

Thank you, Nancy, for rocking the world the way you do with elegance and grace.

{ LESSON 18 }

TRANSITIONS: THE PATH THROUGH PERSONAL CHANGE

by Nancy Meadows

. . . .

As a lifestyle interior designer working with women, life transitions are the reason we initially come together. There are almost always significant transitions that we routinely experience: marriage, divorce, re-marriage, widowhood, downsizing, multigenerational living, aging-in-place, health issues, etc. Every one of these life transitions will directly affect how people live in their homes. My challenge— my passion—is to guide them in such a way that nurtures their best life in this new and unfamiliar place.

When you think about it, we are in stages of transition from the moment of conception to the end of our lives. Life is not static, and we've only to look at nature to see this in action every day. Yet I don't believe we (our society) prepares us well for transitions. We know they exist, but we don't think much about them until the transition occurs, and then it's "Oh boy, how do I deal with this?" The heart races, the stomach churns, and our thoughts become a whirlwind. This occurs even when something we want—something we've worked for—comes to fruition.

RE-THINKING TRANSITIONS

Maybe we need to look at transitions in a different light. Just maybe, if we know they are inevitable, we can change our mindset and begin to embrace them as opportunities. Remember the saying that "If one door closes, another opens." Although trite and overused, it's still true. Or the story of the little boy digging through a pile of manure saying "With all this s--t, there has to be a pony in here somewhere!"

Sometimes transitions are expected. We know our lives will be different when we marry or divorce or have children or change careers. However, there are also those times when life happens while we're busy making other plans.

I'm reminded of a client who was perfectly happy in her home and her career. She was living her life just as she had worked and planned for. Then one day, seemingly out of the blue, she was offered a position that she'd never dreamed of having. The problem? She would have to move to Europe. That meant selling her home, leaving friends and family as well as a job she was happy with, and learning some new skills. In essence, she would be leaving behind everything she knew and was comfortable with.

Did she do it? I'm happy to say she did. Just like Butch Cassidy and the Sundance Kid, she stood at the precipice of the cliff and took the leap. In her case, it was a good choice, and the result of that choice was enriching her life in ways she'd never dreamed of and wouldn't have happened had she not found the courage and belief in herself to take the chance.

Sometimes, we just have to believe we can learn to fly the plane while we're flying it—no matter how scary. If we don't, there's a good chance we will miss out on life's great adventures that allow us to know we're really alive.

I know this is easier for some than others. We're all born with certain genetic dispositions, and the environment in which we were raised plays an equally important role. Yet whether easier or harder, don't we owe it to ourselves to take chances that can only enrich our lives and allow us to live fully? So why then are transitions so scary? Because any transition requires change. In fact, like it or not, change is the only constant we have in this life. It's going to happen whether we want it to or not—whether we feel ready or not.

We get accustomed to the way things are, and then they shift. It's unsettling. I remember an extreme example of this from a true story a child psychologist shared with me. He spoke of a little boy he was treating who had been removed from a dysfunctional family. Although the youngster had suffered great physical and emotional abuse, he was removed from his home literally kicking and screaming. That life was all he knew. It was "normal" for him, and he always knew what to expect. Extreme? Yes, but we all want to do is cling to what we know.

There's a strange kind of comfort with the known. Even positive changes can throw us for a loop. As soon as something nudges us out of our regular routine or challenges our understanding of how the world works and where we fit into it, we're likely to experience a deluge of feelings, including fear, anxiety, sensations of being overwhelmed, distraction, or denial. In turn, those feelings can manifest in behaviors. We might act out with aggressive or passive-aggressive communication. We might push ourselves to overwork or take the opposite approach and procrastinate, avoiding what's on our plate.

THE IMPACT

Our self-care can suffer. We might reach for unhealthy foods and eat too much food or too little. We might neglect physical exercise or not get enough sleep. We might cut ourselves off from others or spend time with people who don't fully support us.

Stress from both positive and negative change can have immediate and long-term effects on our health, our relationships, our work—indeed our very lives. Dealing with inevitable stress in ways that work to our greater good is paramount to living our very best life.

STRATEGIES TO EMBRACE AND PROSPER FROM TRANSITIONS AND CHANGE

Expect setbacks. They are the great teacher. Personal and professional growth is impossible without them. How many times as toddlers did we fall while learning to walk? We just got back up and tried again. Unfortunately, we learn very early in life that to fail is to somehow make us less as a person. Consequently, we back off. We quit, even when we might be just one more try away from success.

Forget perfection. It doesn't exist—not in this world anyway. To expect it can paralyze us from moving successfully forward. Good is good enough, and we keep improving as we move along.

Shifting focus. Albert Einstein said that doing the same thing over and over again and expecting a different outcome is the definition of insanity. While that seems obvious, we've all done it. Sometimes making the smallest adjustment can change everything and reward us with the success we're seeking.

Plan, but don't expect an exact outcome. We never know what delightful twists and turns can occur along the journey. If we're blinded by expectations of an exact outcome, we risk missing out on what could be even better than what we originally thought.

Be passionate. Never underestimate your passion. It's the one thing that keeps us going when the going is toughest. Without it, life is as flat as ginger ale that's lost its fizz. Without passion—whether for people, events, or careers—we're not fully living life as the universe intends us to, and that is with abundance in all things.

Stay aware. With any transition, the way we did things before is different. Our roles change as well, which is the natural order of things. If we marry, we go from single to coupled. If we buy a home, we transition from renter to homeowner. If we change careers, the responsibilities, challenges, and expectations require a different role.

Be proactive. Prepare the best you can for the changes that might come, but then accept the reality of the moment. Think back to other challenges you've overcome, and remind yourself that everything will work out okay this time, too.

FINAL WORDS

We live our lives in chapters. Each chapter carries our story and transitions into the next. The words change. They deepen, they become more enriched, and they weave into a beautiful tapestry that expresses our hopes, dreams, and achievements. That is what can happen when we fully embrace transitions and the changes that result from them.

It's an ongoing process. We're never done. We keep evolving to become our most authentic selves. Every experience—good or bad—can be what propels us forward to the next step in our journey.

Here's the bottom line: Transitions open new and rewarding doors for us. Let change be the catalyst toward your best life. It will feed us in all times, stable or uncertain. We are each unique. No one else thinks or does anything in the same way we do. We all have God-given talents to share with the world and make it a better place for all—and what a blessing that is!

Please accept my gift package which is "Personal Empowerment Through Mindful Interior Design" booklet and "Creating Spaces That Excite Your Senses and Nurture Your Very Best Life" mp 3. www.NancyMeadowsDesigns.com

Miki Strong

Miki Strong is a business strategist and money mentor who shows women how to turn their expertise into thriving businesses. With a keen eye to creating client-attracting profitable offers, she's helped women worldwide build income streams that elevate their lifestyle. Miki's passionate style of support and loving tell-it-to-ya-straight mentorship makes her the go-to-gal for women who are ready to stop playing small and step up to confidently earn their worth. Find out how at **www.mikistrong.com.**

www.mikistrong.com

 www.facebook.com/mikistrong

 www.twitter.com/mikistrong

 www.linkedin.com/in/mikistrong

 www.pinterest.com/mikistrong

Miki is one of the great women I met through some of the joint ventures I organized last year. From the first minute I talked with her, I knew she was highly knowledgeable in regard to money matters, and within minutes she took me on a journey inside my memory. She recalled past experiences that shed light on my own money situation. I was doing well, but I also knew I could do much more. She might not be aware of it, but she gave me a few golden nuggets that day that have stuck with me ever since.

Thank you, Miki, for endorsing the topic of money matters. You have a gift, and I'm honored that you agreed to share it with our readers.

{ LESSON 19 }

FEMININE PRICING POWER: HOW TO CONFIDENTLY STEP INTO LEADERSHIP FOR YOUR CLIENTS, YOUR COLLEAGUES, AND YOUR INDUSTRY BY EARNING YOUR WORTH

by Miki Strong

. . . .

"Behind every successful woman is herself." ~Author unknown

I remember when I first read this quote; it was in the opening chapter of a book similar to the one you're holding in your hands right now. At the time I was being challenged in my business from every direction possible—professionally, creatively, spiritually, and financially. The freedom that drives my business was on a long tropical vacation, and I hadn't been invited. It was a time of financial limitations, fear, doubt, and insecurities. Maybe you can relate.

That quote (and the book) was like balm on my soul, sending the message "You can do this—really do this!" It was the catalyst for banishing my "buts" and making things happen. No one was going to do it for me and I knew—oh, deep down I knew—that this was much bigger than me—and it was time!

WHY IT'S CRITICAL TO GET YOUR MONEY STUFF SORTED OUT

Women are society's glue. We're healers, supporters, champions of the underdog, innovators, big thinkers, and feelers, putting others' needs before our own. We're emotionally wired to connect, which is what makes women extraordinary business leaders.

And if you're in business, you've been called to lead through the work you do, to make a difference in the lives of the people you care about: your family, friends, clients, community, and—yes—even the world. Whether that's your own small corner of the world or maybe you have bigger plans, know that your work does make a difference and that you make a difference, no matter what your "work" is. Your work is your creative expression and how you lead.

No more talking yourself out of what you deserve to be paid.

No more pricing at "just enough to get by."

No more leaving money on the table because you're filled with doubts, fears, and insecurities.

It's time to turn your passion, talents, skills and expertise into profit.

It's time to feel really good about making money because it's a direct reflection of the difference you make.

It's time to own your value and charge your worth.

Because if you're struggling financially, worried about money, or obsessed about earning money, you won't be energetically free to do your great work—the core of your earning potential. So that's what we're going to talk about here: you, in the leadership role of your business, for your clients, your colleagues, and your industry.

Excited? I'm excited for you too!

REMOVING THE BLINDERS OF LOW PRICING SELF-ESTEEM

So what's really going on beneath the challenge of pricing your services, programs, and products—that is, your offers? It's actually quite simple, but first let's talk about what it looks, feels, and sounds like so you know if this is you:

- You compare your prices to those of peers and mentors…and price lower.

- You pack your offers full of content to justify your prices.

- You cringe when you hear "What do you charge?"

- You sometimes discount your fees just to get a client.

- You think "my clients can't afford this."

- You give away too much for free.

- You get tongue-tied and nervous having the money conversation with potential clients.

Girlfriend, this doesn't need to be so hard. What's really going on here is you don't yet understand the value of what you do for your clients—that is, how you impact their lives. You see, up until now, you might have thought your work is about you.

It's not. It's about the people you serve.

Feminine Pricing Power: Value the impact you have on your clients' lives.

WHAT YOUR PRICES SAY

Think about the last time you were looking to buy a product or hire someone for a service. You looked at the price and instantly made a judgment, right? If the price was outside your comfort zone, you thought it was too high. Or maybe you thought it was too low and questioned the value—after all, you get what you pay for. If you bought it, you thought the price was just right.

Do you know what made you decide to buy? The perceived value of the product or service matched the price you were willing to pay to get the result you were looking for. (You might want to read that again.)

Your prospective clients do the same thing. Price too low and they'll question the value of what they receive; price too high—without communicating the value of your offer—and they'll think you overcharge. Price your offers to communicate "I am confident that what I do and what I have to offer will help you get what you want" and your clients will pay you what you are worth—and love you for it!

Feminine Pricing Power: Price from confidence in your expertise.

WHAT YOUR CLIENTS ARE REALLY PAYING YOU FOR

You might think your clients pay for your uber-cool process, secret steps, charming personality, or clever words. They don't. Your clients pay you to help them get to the "XYZ" result, period!

What you're really selling is a result—an emotional result. You're selling how your clients will feel when they use your product or hire your services. That's why it's critical to know your ideal client—and not in the niche or "this is the group of people I serve" kind of way. What I'm talking about is getting intimate with the person you're ideally suited to serve.

Personalize. For instance, if you serve women, think of her as an individual—know her deepest desires, most pressing wants, and unmet needs. Know her heart and her mind. Know what she values and what's most important to her. Know what she thinks about, talks about, and what she thinks about but will never talk about (but secretly wishes you will). Know her struggles and what she's challenged with.

Then create a solution—one solution to one challenge in one offer.

Feminine Pricing Power: Be a problem-solver for your clients.

K.I.S.S. YOUR GREAT WORK

A colleague and mentor I admire says "Keep It Strategically Simple." I love this acronym because simplicity is the center of every effective system. Your great work is like that: It's what you do very well, comes easy to you, and fills you up.

The trap we women fall into is thinking that, to be successful in business, we must be all things to all people. After all, we don't want to leave anyone out. It's just not so. You can help many more people by putting your energy into cultivating your expertise.

Think about it: When you love what you do, you're naturally inclined to get better at it. You'll read books on the subject, sign up for training, implement what you learn, and actively find ways to improve your craft. You'll get better results for your clients. Your kiss of success comes from matching your expertise with creating solutions for your clients.

Feminine Pricing Power: Your clients pay for your expertise, not your credentials.

HOW TO PRICE LIKE A LEADER

It's time to step fully into leadership by engaging your feminine pricing power. How you show up here sets the example for how your clients will value themselves. Understand that, when they hire you or buy your products or programs, they're really investing in themselves.

Feminine Pricing Power Guidelines

1. Price your expertise (how effectively you get clients to the result they're looking for), not your credentials, training, certification, or years of experience.

2. Know your market and what their pricing comfort zone is. Yes, it's okay to stretch it, but don't price yourself out of your market. If your prices are too high for your community, it's likely you need to revisit your ideal client. Price too low, and you can turn off potential clients.

3. Personal time is premium, so any 1-to-1 services will merit a higher fee. You're with me on this, yes?

4. Be consistent and intentional in your pricing. Resist the urge to pick a price because it sounds good or because it's what your peers charge. Know what you're pricing and why.

5. Make it easy to say yes by including payment plans on your higher-priced offers. To do this, add an additional percentage to the price of the offer to cover additional fees and the risk you carry.

6. Provide peace of mind by standing behind your offers: Give guarantees or clearly state your policy on returns, refunds, and exchanges.

7. Review your pricing annually. As your expertise grows, consider raising your prices.

The buck stops (and starts) here. You've got to feel good about your prices for your clients to feel confident in hiring you. Start where you are right now and increase your prices just outside your comfort zone. Gradually increase until you're charging what you're worth and loving it!

Patty Farmer

Patty Farmer, The Networking CEO™, is an award-winning and in-demand marketing and social media strategist, professional speaker, radio show host, and co-author of the highly acclaimed book *Make Your Connections Count*. A consummate community builder, Patty founded BizLink Networking, a national face-to-face professional business networking organization, and BizLink Global, an online B2B referral, networking, and education center. We invite you to join the BizLink Global community at **www.BizLinkGlobal.com.**

www.PattyFarmer.com

www.Facebook.com/PattyFarmerCEO

www.Twitter.com/PattyFarmer

www.LinkedIn.com/in/pattyfarmer

· ·

Patty is a real connector. She knows how to network like the back of her hand, and what is really amazing is how elegantly she does it. I met Patty through a little program we both belonged to. Being a true collaborator herself, it was meant to be for both of us to participate in a joint venture together.

Thank you, Patty, for being part of this project despite your heavy schedule. I know it was not easy, but I'm so grateful you found the time to do it. I had to cover collaboration, and I knew you were the person to do it.

{ LESSON 20 }

TRANSFORM YOUR NETWORKING TO CREATE CASH-GENERATING COLLABORATIONS

by Patty Farmer

. . . .

Imagine you're getting ready for a networking event with an expected attendance of 150 people. You've showered, chosen your outfit, put your makeup on, gathered your business cards and nametag—all your tools for success are in place. As you're getting ready, you're thinking about what you're going to say and how you'll pitch your products and services. You're excited to get there.

Now stop and ask yourself whether you're thinking, "I can't wait to hear what the other 149 people have to sell" or are you thinking "I can't wait to tell 149 people what I have to sell!"

If all 150 people are thinking about how they want to talk to everyone else about their products and services and no one is thinking they just can't wait to hear what everyone else has to sell, how can this possibly be a successful event? Will you walk away thinking you did exactly what you came here to do?

When you're talking, will the other person just be waiting for you to pause so they can start pitching their business, products, or services? Or maybe they will ask the age-old question: "So what do you do?" How you answer this question is very important. Typically when people answer this question, they either start pitching or very literally tell exactly what they do.

What if we could change the outcome of the entire event with a slight mindset shift - by simply changing the question? So let's rewind a little bit. Let's go back to getting ready for the event. . Go ahead and gather those same tools of success, only this time think, "I can't wait to listen to what the other 149 people say so I can find out if they serve the same target market I do, if there's some synergy, or if there's an opportunity to collaborate."

Instead of asking "what do you do?" with the predictable outcome, let's shift our questions slightly for a more productive outcome.

"Who do you serve?" or *"What industries do you serve?"*

Changes the whole dynamic, right? Now you're finding out whether you serve the same target market. You might discover that your product or service can be repackaged for a different target market. Maybe they serve your target market in a completely different way that opens up all kinds of collaborative opportunity. You might find out you know someone who is looking for their services, that you can be instrumental in introducing them and they'll be able to collaborate. After all, networking is all about being of service.

"What's the most interesting project you're working on right now and how can I help?"

It's really great to see what lights others up. You might now be able to start a relationship around something they're passionate about. Remember, it's really about opening up relationships rather than closing sales. Relationships are the currency of the current business climate.

"I meet lots of people. What should I be listening for that will let me know I should introduce them to you?"

You will discover the value others bring to their customers and gain clarity about what they do. You will also learn how you can be of service to them as well as your contacts who might need those products or services. This can help you identify collaborative opportunities.

In addition to traditional local networking, other ways you organically meet people in the course of doing business are equally great ways to find collaborative partners. We tend to gravitate toward places our prospects are gathered or to relevant information. LinkedIn groups and Google+ Hangouts are a great way to see where your target market congregates online. Take a look at the magazines you read and your Google Reader. From national conferences and professional association meetings to social media and blogs you enjoy reading, identify the influencers and key people you'd like to collaborate with globally.

There are many ways to collaborate—joint webinars, teleseminars, live events, guest blogging, podcasts, speaking opportunities, lunch and learns, or hosting a call with an expert for your target market. You can co-create a product or put together a complementary service package. Get creative and broaden your view of what would truly add value for your customer base. For example, a mortgage broker might decide to put on a first-time buyer seminar with the expected partners—realtors, title companies, and insurance agents—then take it a step further with a credit repair specialist.

Once you identify a potential partner and project, you can begin to experience the benefits of collaboration. When you open your rolodex to each other (not giving it away), you each have the potential to expand your lists, gain referrals, and increase your web traffic. Opt-in marketing (where you provide valuable information in exchange for permission to use their contact information to interact with them) is a good way to build your list and begin the process of building relationships with your new prospects.

You'll expand your connections and influence as well as build credibility. You might be able to cut costs by sharing expenses. In a group project like a teleseminar, you can get to know the other people your partner collaborates with and find other potential collaborative partners. Look for the win-win-win—opportunities that are good for each of you plus add value for your audience.

When you're choosing collaborative partners, don't forget to do your due diligence. Thoroughly research the reputation of your potential collaborative partner to be sure you'd be comfortable with it as an extension of your reputation.

Be sure to clearly define expectations upfront. Put an agreement in writing that states what you both bring to the table, how you will promote the event, etc. Be clear about how each party will accomplish their duties and how conflicts will be resolved. Include an exit strategy in case things don't go as agreed. This will ensure that things go as you envision with the best possible results for all involved.

Asking the right questions will help you to open up your mind, open up your list, and expand your horizons. If everyone came to networking events expecting to actively listen to what others are doing and for opportunities that might exist to work together, the possibilities would be limitless. Go into your next event with this new strategy and you will win-win-win!

EXERCISE:

Step 1: Identify a gap in your product or service offerings to your customers.

Step 2: Explore how you'd like to expand your customer base.

Step 3: Look for a credible, experienced partner who offers complementary products or services and has the type of customers you'd like to add to your customer base. Look back on the last three events you attended. (Maybe you even have a stack of business cards sitting on your desk waiting for you to follow up on.) Are there people you met whom you can reconnect with to determine whether collaboration opportunities exist? It helps to look at networking as a series of conversations.

Step 4: List five open-ended questions you will use to get to know your contacts' businesses, target markets, and current projects.

Step 5: Reach out to the contacts you've identified and start the conversation by phone, email, or social media. Happy collaborating!

Ava Diamond

Ava Diamond, founder of Big Impact Speaking, works with big vision entrepreneurs to increase their income, influence, and impact through speaking.

She draws on her 17 years as a professional speaker to help her clients laser-focus their message, craft their signature talk, deliver it powerfully from the stage, get all the clients they want, and become known as the "go-to" expert in their fields.

Download your free "Rock Your Speaking Power Pack" at
http://bigimpactspeaking.com

✉ **ava@bigimpactspeaking.com**

🅕 **facebook.com/BigImpactSpeaking**

🅕 **facebook.com/avadiamond**

🅣 **twitter.com/feistywoman**

🅛 **linkedin.com/in/avadiamond**

. . . .

Ava is not only a wonderful public speaker, but she is also a terrific communicator. I had the great pleasure of speaking with her over Skype, and I got to meet a really vibrant and passionate woman.

Thank you, Ava, for being willing to share your unique brilliance with the world.

{ LESSON 21 }

CHANGE THE WORLD...ONE AUDIENCE AT A TIME

by Ava Diamond

. . . .

You have the power to change the world! Through speaking, you can shift what people believe about themselves, their businesses and their lives. You can awaken them to new possibilities and show them the path to get there. You can alter the course of peoples' lives. And you can get all of the clients you want.

Today's world calls us to be real, be authentic, and be fully in our power. Each of us has an individual combination of gifts, talents, life experiences, and lessons learned that make our message, what we offer and how we serve unique. Revealing and standing in the power of your own magnificence gives you the ability to inspire and impact thousands of people.

It is up to each of us to bring our message forth to serve the world—one audience at a time. Then we can work with people from these audiences beyond the speech to help them transform their lives.

> "When I dare to be powerful, to use my strength in the service of my vision, then it becomes less and less important whether I am afraid."
> ~Audre Lorde

STEPPING INTO YOUR BIG MESSAGE

"But Ava, what would I talk about? And who would want to listen to me? There is so much marketing noise out there—how will I stand out?" These are some of the most common questions clients ask me.

Your message comes from the deepest part of you—from your heart and soul. It comes from the challenges you've faced and overcome, from the obstacles you've gotten though, from the lessons you've learned as you've lived your life. It's the answer to the questions: "What is really meaningful to me? What message needs to come through me? "What am I compelled to share with the world?" That's what you share...your passion, your voice, and your heart-centered message.

OWNING YOUR POWER

I've noticed an interesting thing with a few of my private clients over the last few months. Our coaching sessions have been less about creating their actual speech, and more about coaching them in stepping into their power, really owning their message, and shifting their mindset about who they are and what they have to offer.

They have been playing small. They have been reluctant to step out in a big way, charge what they're worth, and let people see the highly powerful transformation that they can provide.

Your playing small serves no one! It doesn't serve you. It doesn't serve the people you can help.

You are here for a reason. You decided to become a coach, a healer, an entrepreneur, a speaker because you are passionate about what you can offer people. You are passionate about how you can help. You are passionate about transforming lives.

Yet for many people, although they have this desire within them they hold themselves back. They suffer from "comparison-itis." They compare themselves to other speakers, decide they're "not as good as so and so," and sabotage themselves in small ways that add up to big damage.

They are reluctant to reach out and book speaking gigs. They're afraid to be really powerful on stage. They don't step into their message in a big way.

Or they have a self image that makes them ask themselves, "Who do you think you are to claim expert status and put yourself out here?"

They lack confidence—and that comes across to their audiences.

Remember, your ideal client is struggling. They are having problems and challenges that impact their businesses and their lives. You have a solution to their problem. You can be the bridge from their struggle to their dream.

And if you hold yourself back, it you don't "own it" and get out and share your message and offer your services, you deny them the opportunity to get the transformation you offer. You're withholding their solution because of your own fear. Their lives don't get better because you are playing small.

There's never been a better time to stand in your power, to own your expertise, to play a bigger game, and to offer your ideal client your transformation. People need your message. They need you to have the courage, the passion, and the drive to be a powerful messenger and to bring them solutions.

BECOMING A THOUGHT LEADER

To become a thought leader, you need a laser focused message. You have to let go of the strategy of "hedging your bets," of "being all things to all people so you don't miss out on any opportunties." You can't serve everyone—nor should you! You want to focus on the one thing you do best—and focus on the group of people who need it the most.

When is the last time you booked time in your calendar just to think? When is the last time you purposely examined your assumptions and moved beyond your current thinking? When is the last time you commtted to innovating in your field?

Here's a great method of solidifying your original thinking that I learned from my colleage Neen James at a National Speakers Association meeting. Take the top 3 books in your field. Then, have two pads, one labeled, "Yes, and...", and one labeled "Yes, but." Go through each book. Take a point in a book, then say to yourself, "Yes, and..." or "Yes, but," and write down your original ideas. This will help you solidify your own thinking, and identify where you think beyond or contrary to what's out there. This will help you identify your thought leadership.

Then, get out and share your deep expertise and your original thinking. This separates you from the hordes who are "just a commodity." When you're a commodity, you're an "also," you can't charge premium pricing, and you'll be fighting for mindspace and attention in the marketplace.

When you're a thought leader, there is no competition, people are clamoring to work with you, and you are the go-to person in your field.

ATTRACTING MORE CLIENTS

You are doing your audience a disservice if you don't offer them a way to take the learning further. Think about it. Your audience has a problem they're struggling with. It's having a negative impact on their lives or their businesses—or both. You have a solution for them. You know how to help them.

You give them what you can in the half hour or hour you have with them, but you know so much more than you could ever share in the short time you have together. You have a process that will help them fix their problem.

So if you don't give them an opportunity to work with you further, to get the solution to their problem, you really are not serving them.

You owe it to your audience to become great at making offers. You owe it to them to open up the possibility in their lives of having their problem solved. You owe it to them to give them a way to work with you so that their businesses and their lives will be better.

When you come from this place—of service, of helping, of offering a solution to something they're struggling with—and you do so with authenticity and passion and authority, your sales will skyrocket and you'll have all the clients you want. You're just giving them a chance to say yes to themselves. And that's the greatest gift you can give to your audiences.

7 STEPS TO GREAT SPEAKING

1. **Know your ideal client.** Know them intimately. Know what they're struggling with, what keeps them up at night, what problem they'll pay money to solve.

2. **Know how you can be the path or the bridge** from their problem to their dream—to their solution.

3. **Think big.** Be willing to step into this bigger idea of who you are, what you can offer, and how it will be transformational for people.

4. **Get scared.** If that bigger idea doesn't scare you, it's not big enough. Feel the fear. Let it excite you—because it's a sign that you're moving out of your comfort zone and into the zone where magic happens.

5. **Laser-focus your message.** It needs to be crystal clear for your ideal clients and your audiences.

6. **Get good. Do whatever it takes to develop your speaking skills.** Hire a coach, find a mentor, read, study, practice, get feedback. All of these things are helpful. Develop a killer signature talk.

7. **Get out there. Share your message.** Give people the opportunity to work with you. Get good at selling from the stage. You can't help people if they don't sign up to work with you.

Being a powerful speaker starts with your own mindset and your own beliefs. I invite you to step into your power, share your message, and have a big impact!

APPLICATION EXERCISE:

What if you could only give one speech, and it could only be one minute long? What would you share with that audience? What's your big message—the thing that sets you on fire? Writing that that one minute speech will help you get clear and laser-focused.

Lisa Rothstein

Lisa Rothstein is an award-winning copywriter and marketing strategist whose advertising agency clients include IBM, Colgate, Hanes, and many more. She created the famous "Wait'll We Get Our Hanes on You" campaign that turned underwear into fashion. Lisa now works as a business coach, copywriter, and "idea person" for high-end creative entrepreneurs and businesses worldwide. She is also a sought-after speaker. Find out more or book a free consult at www.lisarothstein.com. Join Lisa's free webinar: **www.easycopywebinar.com**.

f **http://www.facebook.com/yourcreativeconsultant**

f **http://www.facebook.com/thelisarothstein**

y **http://www.twitter.com/davincidiva**

in **http://www.linkedin.com/in/yourwriterforhire**

p **http://pinterest.com/rothsteinlisa**

. . . .

I first met Lisa through a Facebook group we both belong to and I really liked her ideas and the way she uses copyrighting as a tool to help women entrepreneurs. So, needless to say, when I was looking for someone to cover this particular topic, she was my first choice.

Thank you so much, Lisa, for allowing me to showcase the importance of copywriting in the equation of success.

{ LESSON 22 }

GOOD COPYWRITING IN YOUR BUSINESS: WHY IT MATTERS AND HOW TO CREATE IT YOURSELF

by Lisa Rothstein

. . . .

Forget the economy. It's the new Gold Rush out there in Internet-land. Any entrepreneur with a good idea and a product or service that has value to anyone can hang out her shingle and write her own ticket. Because unlike the old days of mainstream Madison Avenue advertising, today you don't need a multi-million-dollar Super Bowl commercial to get noticed. Technology like WordPress and Facebook means that anyone can have as good a presence as an IBM or a Coca-Cola in the media people pay most attention to these days, for less than the price of a good dinner out.

Although you don't need a big ad agency or a mammoth budget, you do need one thing the big boys have: good copywriting. In fact, now that everyone can have the same media, your message matters more than ever. Here's why:

1. Your copy is your ambassador. It's also your publicity agent and your defense attorney. It stands in for you and has to convince people of your value on its own.

2. It's how you speak to the many, not just the one. With the internet, your copy could be seen by thousands of people, so that first impression better be a good one.

3. It's how your potential joint venture partners form their opinions of you. These days, everyone checks you out online

first before they'd ever dream of doing business with you.

4. It is the only way to cut through the clutter. The power of a good idea—and the words that clearly express it—are the only things that will get noticed and keep the attention of your customer in this noisy world.

5. It will make you a lot more money than mediocre copy. You're not in business to win literary awards. Good copy is good because it works. That's why top copywriters can command $10,000 and more for a single online sales page.

Unfortunately, there are a few obstacles nearly all entrepreneurs face when getting good copy written for their businesses. First, they think it's necessary to hire a high-priced copywriter right out of the gate. While a "hired gun" copywriter can be a smart investment for established business owners, it's not appropriate for someone new, who might not yet have the audience traffic or the prices to make it pay.

Yet when new entrepreneurs try to do their own copy, they often feel hopelessly inadequate. They think they can't because they are not "a writer" or they don't know the secret tricks of the trade or because the blank page or screen is paralyzing and they don't know where to start.

Some business owners make the mistake of copying other companies, adopting a needlessly highbrow corporate tone or vocabulary. This only serves to make their message inauthentic, pompous, and—ultimately—ineffective.

The good news is that anyone can have great copy for their business. It just takes a bit of practice, plus a healthy dose of common sense.

The number one way to have copy that works is not to worry about copy as much as about your client. Articulate her problems and desires so clearly and demonstrate such a deep understanding that she thinks you know her. When you are able to explain what's wrong or missing in her life better than she can—when she says, "That's it! This person (or company) really gets me!"—then you are light-years closer to a sale.

The irony is, if you do this, it almost does not matter what you are selling. People buy for reasons that have less to do with the intrinsic value of the product than what it stands for. Think of Apple or Mercedes-Benz products. Both cost many times more than their competition. If you took them apart, would the value of their components be that much more? Of course not. Then what's the difference? The way they understand and "feed back" their buyers' needs, desires, and dreams makes their product seem like the only choice.

This is the first step of a "magical" 5-step copywriting process I first learned fresh out of college as a junior copywriter at Young & Rubicam, one of the world's top ad agencies. I still use it to write copy for my clients, and so can you. I call it the 1.) "Oh, Dear!" 2.) "Good News!" 3.) "Here's Why…" 4.) "That's Right!" and 5.) "But Wait! There's…MORE!" copywriting process, and once you know it, you'll start seeing it everywhere.

"Oh Dear!" is where you identify and "dimensionalize" the problem. It's the "ring-around-the-collar," "I've-got-a-headache," "diets-never-work," "my-sex-life-is-nonexistent," "I'm-jealous-of-the-other-guy" cry for help. Even if your product or service just solves a little problem, shining a light on it can make it seem like an urgent crisis (and they'll be nodding in recognition, saying, "I hate when that happens!").

Then comes "Good News!" Your product or service is here to save the day! It is designed to fix that very problem. Here's where you describe what life will look like once they've gotten it and everything is great. You might even describe the "end-end" benefits, extra goodies that they will receive as a result of their main problem having been solved. You can show how your solution for business has positive ripple effects in other areas, such as health, relationships, and overall well-being as well as their finances.

But now they may think it's too good to be true. That's when you come in with the "Here's Why…" section. "Here's why" covers a lot: Here's why they can believe you—you show other people who have gotten results. Here's why it works—you show a demonstration or explain the process. Sometimes you'll have a story: Here's why

I created this solution—because I was in the same place you are and I made it for myself. Of course there's the "Here's why you'll be satisfied—it comes with all this stuff," where you outline all the features and more benefits for each. And "Here's why there's no risk to you"—because you give a guarantee.

"That's right" is where you recap and add up everything they will get: their problem solved, the amazing result, all the benefits and all the features, and how valuable (maybe even in specific dollar terms) they all are. They get all this at a price that should now look like the bargain of the century in comparison.

That's the end of the copy story for most mainstream advertising. The last "magic phrase" is reserved for direct marketing like infomercials and online sales letters, and you already know it: "But wait….there's MORE!"

This is where you'll add extra value to your already great deal to make it a real "no-brainer." This is where infomercials say they'll double your offer, give you free shipping, or throw in a valuable bonus product with your purchase. Often the bonuses will appear even more attractive than the original offer, and people will buy just to get it. A secret tip is that sometimes advertisers take a feature out of the original product and reserve it as a "bonus" so that it will feel more valuable. Another trick is to include something as a bonus that costs little or nothing to deliver, but is of great value to the customer, such as a digital product or even a physical one you've got in overstock.

These five phrases—Oh Dear, Good News, Here's Why, That's Right, and But Wait, There's More—are all you need to get started creating good solid sales copy for your business. Like a painter, you won't use all the colors in your palette in the same way each time, but you'll be glad to have them all to create a complete picture.

Margo DeGange

Margo DeGange, M.Ed., author and international speaker, is a business and lifestyle designer and founder of WomenOfSplendor. com, the exciting mentoring organization where women collaborate, develop their brilliance, increase their reach and visibility, and bring healing to the world in a big way! Discover your "Gift of Brilliance" and shine full throttle through Margo's products, programs, mastermind training, and free gifts at MargoDeGange.com.

For content-rich facilitator training to run prosperous mastermind groups and programs, visit **MargoDeGange.com/mastermind-training**

http://www.MargoDeGange.com
http://www.WomenOfSplendor.com

✉ Margo@MargodeGange.com

𝐟 http://www.Facebook.com/MargoDeGange

𝐟 http://www.Facebook.com/YourBusinessCoach

𝐟 http://www.Facebook.com/WomenOfSplendor

🐦 http://www.Twitter.com/MargoDeGange @MargoDeGange

🐦 http://www.Twitter.com/WomenOfSplendor @WomenOfSplendor

in http://www.Linkedin.com/in/margodegange

📌 http://www.Pinterest.com/MargoDeGange

📌 http://www.Pinterest.com/WomenofSplendor

Okay, where should I start? Margo is Margo: She is a true friend, a shoulder, a terrific brainstormer, a compassionate mastermind leader, and a ball of energy (Italian meatballs), but also—and above all—Margo is a giver of love.

Thank you, Margo, for just being you. Without you, this book wouldn't exist. You are the one who helped me put one foot forward by saying to my "unprocessed" DM: "Fantastic, I'm in!" You are one of a kind, and your clients are blessed.

{ LESSON 23 }

WILD SUCCESS THROUGH
MASTERMIND BRILLIANCE

by Margo DeGange, M.Ed.

. . . .

"If a small group of ladies got together weekly to shoot the
bull, no telling what unproductive crud might come up, but
if that same group gathered with good intentions and a clear
and definite purpose, they could actually change the world"
~Margo DeGange

Did you know that there is a giant, super cool mind that floats around
all of us at all times? Yep! It's called the MASTER-mind (or source)
and ladies you can tap into that mastermind for over-the-top, life-
changing, business-building success!

You sure can, and I'm going to tell you exactly how to gather with a
motivated peer group to exponentially accelerate your growth. Yes,
without being a mathematician, you can substantially increase your
rate of advancement through what is known as a mastermind group!

Right here, right now, I'm showing up for you in this priceless little
book to inspire you and get you really excited about your life—about
the splendid opportunities and possibilities just waiting for you in a
mastermind.

What is a mastermind? I've got the inside scoop. I will tell you and
then show you—step-by-high-heel-step—how to create your very
own mastermind group (to lead or join—whichever tickles your toes)
so you can catapult into mind-blowing success.

Glow-ry!

You are here in the world for a glorious purpose, with a big and important mission to accomplish through your extraordinary life-work. A mastermind group is just the thing to help you do it full throttle!

Okay, ladies, here's how it's gonna go down:

- First, I'll present you with Your Mastermind Lesson to answer your compelling questions and give you a great foundation on which to build.

- Next, I'll make you privy to my must-have Mastermind Mindset Tips for solid thinking that drives you from love and abundance.

- Finally, I'll conclude with Your Mastermind Action Exercise so you can start your very own mastermind group right away—one you'll infuse with your own style and your own crazy kinda love! This is business for the soul!

I'll approach your lesson and mindset tips so they relate to you whether you're leading or participating in a group. I'll approach your action exercise as if you are leading (you can tweak it if you're not). So strap up your stilettos and let's get moving!

YOUR MASTERMIND LESSON

"Empower your business through the brilliance of great minds!" ~Me!

I'll tell you straight up: There are many types of masterminds, and we can't go into them all here, but once you get your pedicured feet wet, you'll get creative and design your own custom groups. I've helped scores of individuals create programs to fit their personalities and their brilliant messages, but for now, we'll keep it simple.

Let's focus on a mastermind I created for my tribe called the Think-Tank Mastermind. Here, group members serve as "thinkers" to inspire ideas, support, strategy, and growth. I run several of these each year, and they work fabulously for both beginners and seasoned professionals.

SO WHAT IN THE HIGH-HEELS IS A MASTERMIND, ANYWAY?

A mastermind is a group of highly motivated individuals who meet regularly with a commitment to grow and succeed. Each group member works toward her own personal or professional growth while also working for the advancement and success of the others. The overall group purpose is to create **momentum** and **forward motion** so each member can accomplish her most significant goals and realize her most meaningful dreams.

The all-inspiring premise is that, when we collaborate within a harmonious and intentionally aligned group of peers, we access that powerful source-energy to generate marvelously divine ideas, innovations, and solutions that would never have been accessed otherwise. The ideal objective is to create synergy, where the combined effort of the group is greater than that of the individual parts.

For individual group members, the work is to identify specific goals in line with a clear and inspiring vision and create effective strategy to reach those goals. Then, based on the strategy, a set of focused, consistent, and directed actions (tactics) can be identified to move forward in life, business, or career. The ultimate goal is to advance and thrive, making a greater impact in the world.

MORE GROOVY BENEFITS OF A MASTERMIND!

There are more benefits to a mastermind than shoes in a rock star's closet! The top benefit is that, through clarity of focus, you'll get in a rapid-fire zone of motion and momentum, working strategically on the very things that matter most, while side-stepping distractions that would otherwise throw you off course.

Another key benefit is that group work frees you from the isolation you might otherwise experience without regular access to colleagues and networks.

The perks don't stop there. Include in your benefits package confidantes who'll challenge and inspire you with creative ideas, off-the-charts brainstorming, amazing marketing tactics, time-saving strategies, heart-felt support, and tenacious (but gentle) accountability. You'll make quality, lifelong friendships, too. Plus, you'll tap into new and incredible resources you never knew existed!

HOW IT WORKS

Meeting formats vary. For the Think-Tank Mastermind I run, there is a facilitator (leader) and members in a nonjudgmental environment. The facilitator opens the meeting with a greeting and short message, and she recaps key highlights from the last meeting. She then systematically opens the floor to each member, giving them an allotted amount of time to be in what is called the "Hot Seat."

In the Hot Seat, a member shares a problem, challenge, question, or idea she needs help or support with. When a member is through sharing, the facilitator opens the floor to feedback from other members, who offer positive, supportive, insights, solutions, and resources with the goal of helping the member in the Hot Seat decide on a next-step action. When that member's time is up, another member takes the Hot Seat until all members have gone. For this type of mastermind, the group size should be small.

MASTERMIND MINDSET TIPS

"Baseball is 90% mental, the other half is physical." ~Yogi Berra

Whether you're shopping for shoes, playing baseball, or running a business, success is 90% mindset. Get your thinking straight and you're just about home. With that, here's the bottom-line skinny on getting your thinking in order—12 crucial mindset tips for mastermind brilliance and success!

1. Intentions

Know why you are there. Align both your actions and attitudes with sincere and honest motives that are best for the group. Set an umbrella intention for your overall participation, then set a specific intention for each meeting.

2. Goals

What do you want to accomplish? Where do you need help? Before each meeting, have a specific goal in mind. Don't waste mastermind time floundering. Get as clear as you can in advance.

3. Motion

Forward motion is the entire point of a mastermind, so come ready to work and ready to move forward.

4. Discomfort

Get comfy being uncomfortable. When challenged, we grow! At times, you're going to feel stretched. If you want success, get used to it!

5. Sloppiness

Don't flop into your meetings sloppy and unprepared. Enter with your power switch "on"!

6. Empowerment

This is a no-therapy zone! A mastermind group isn't the "couch" for dealing with emotional scars, issues, and resentments. Discover your own empowerment and function from it so you reach greater levels of enrichment and achievement.

7. Accountability and Responsibility

Your peers have invested time and money and expect full throttle responsibility and accountability. Nothing less will fly.

8. Muck

You've joined a mastermind group to move into your brilliance. Still, a little muck will come up from time to time, with sparkly tears to match—it's all part of the growth process! What's not part of the process is staying muck-stuck or focusing on the negative. The muck should push you forward. It's not there for wallowing.

9. Integrity

Integrity's tied to intention. For mastermind brilliance, each member must matter greatly to all other members. Be generous with ideas and resources to help your peers leap forward. Don't be greedy with the goodies!

10. Commitment

Make up your mind that you're in this through thick and thin and for the long haul. Be on time for meetings, and do all you can to honor meeting dates.

11. Harmony

Harmony is vital to mastermind success. Without it, you won't turn on that invisible energy force-field that fuels exponential growth. In a group, occasionally you'll have to overcome negative thoughts, such as "I don't like her style" or "they're way ahead of me" or "I can't believe she said that!" These thoughts are natural, but choose not to embrace thoughts that trouble you or divide you from others.

12. Source Energy

A mastermind works on a spiritual level to tap into source energy, where all thought is creative and positive. Source energy is released when we determine to help each member of our group as we would help ourselves. This creates a space where ideas and amazing solutions flow, and the rate of growth increases. That is the real power of the mastermind!

YOUR MASTERMIND ACTION EXERCISE

"It's not enough to have a great idea. You've got to make that great idea happen!" ~Me again!

Okay, you're now good to go and ready to take action. Step out in your swanky high-heels and make it happen.

Here's a 10-Step No-Bull Plan to lead your own mastermind group right away!:

1. Decide on a topic, like business growth or self-care.

2. Name your mastermind to capture its essence and purpose, such as "Purposeful Life-design Mastermind" or "Creative Marketing Mastermind."

3. Fee or free? I fully believe that when members are financially invested, they take greater responsibility and they experience greater success.

4. Determine group size: 3-8 is good. My Think-Tank Masterminds are 4-8 people.

5. Decide when and how often your group will meet. Include a start and end date, and set all dates in advance. I suggest meeting once or twice a month.

6. Determine the length of meetings. I recommend 90 minutes to two hours depending on the group's size.

7. Decide where you'll meet. Set up the venue in advance. Meet locally at a home, office, or hotel or nationally/internationally by phone through a conference bridge line.

8. Create a basic agenda for your meetings. Your first call will be a get aquatinted session (different from subsequent meetings). For a sample agenda of each, go to **margodegange.com/sample-mastermind-agendas** (my gift to you)!

9. Create marketing materials like a simple .PDF with the details and/or a sales page.

10. Invite your peeps! Send your .PDF to past clients and colleagues by invitation only with a VIP price. Then reach out to your list and social media tribe.

Kathleen Hanagan

Kathleen Hanagan, business coach, psychotherapist, and speaker, helps purpose-driven entrepreneurs claim their brilliance, clarify their message, and make the money to fulfill their mission, without betraying their hearts. With her wisdom, warmth, and laser focus, Kathleen helps you clear away the debris of the past and connect to your vision, which resets an inner compass toward your highest destiny. This alignment makes you a magnet for the love and success you deeply desire.

www.TurnOnYourLight.com

 Kathleen@TurnOnYourLight.com

. . . .

Kathleen is one of the women I got to meet through my Facebook network (I hope you are getting the idea that Facebook is not a waste of time when you know how to use it). Kathleen is covering con brio the subject of love. My mission for 2013 is to only do what I love with people I love. Why? Because after so many years of being in business, I realized that it is the only way to truly be successful and happy in your life and, therefore, in your business. You can feel love in every word used in Kathleen's chapter. I'm so honored to have a chapter covering such a crucial subject.

Thank you, Kathleen, for accepting the challenge of writing this sumptuous chapter while having so little time to spare. I really appreciate it.

{ LESSON 24 }

THERE IS NO SUCCESS WITHOUT LOVE
by Kathleen Hanagan

. . . .

"Your task is not to seek for love, but merely to seek and
find all of the barriers within yourself that you have built
against it." ~A Course in Miracles

I had already proven myself to be a successful, professional woman
who lived in a magnificent home near Washington, D.C., called "The
Temple," where many people came for healing and transformation.
I served as a psychotherapist/priestess/poet, had already raised 3
remarkable children, and wanted for nothing financially. But at 57,
the familiar restlessness began to stir, and I was called on once again
make some sweeping changes that would bring me face to face with
my biggest fears, hidden well by the guise of success.

The seeds of this change were planted in a powerful vision I had
while living in the Andes in 2005. I had closed my practice and moved
to Cusco, Peru, where I lived and explored the shamanic realm for a
year. Although I did not have the consciousness at that time to fully
understand the vision, my poetry was prophetic of what was to come.
Here are some lines from *The Universe Holds Its Breath*:

Over and over

you bear witness to this Presence

holding its breath

until it breathes through you

as if you matter

in the grand scheme of things.

I felt in my very bones how utterly significant each person is in the grand scheme of things and that the work I had been doing for years with 1 or 2 people in my office needed to expand. Having spent years struggling with my own feelings of insignificance, I was well-equipped to help others claim their true worth. I saw in the vision that, when each person's light shines as bright as it can be, the illusion of darkness would be lifted. I knew I myself needed to shine a brighter light with more reach.

I closed my practice, sold my beautiful home, and moved back to New England, where I had grown up. I immersed myself in deep soul-searching for many months until it was clear to me that I was being called to assist in the unfolding of a new economy, which would be fundamental for the New Earth. Once I decided, I was determined to be successful.

I learned everything I could about marketing and the countless tasks involved in building a business both online and off. I did my best to keep up with it all. In the process, I became exhausted and began to compare myself to some of the most successful entrepreneurs in the business, devaluing my own skill and worth as a result.

I felt small and insignificant and realized that it was not the first time I had faced such feelings. This new work was bringing up all my insecurities.

I started to push harder. I was focused on getting things done at the expense of my joy and even my health at times. I found myself skipping my morning meditation to launch into emails, which never stopped coming. I began to dread every day as just another grind, an endless list of things to do.

Forget relationships. I had no time. All my years of working with the body and sacred sexuality seemed like another life. I lived at my computer. I listened to a teleclass while walking, driving, or cooking. So much to do, and so much suffering!

Fear was driving my very existence. There was all this talk about mindset in the entrepreneurial community, and I had been teaching it for years, but somehow, I had lost my way. None of that seemed to work for me now.

163

A RETURN TO THE VISION

Michael Beckwith said, "The pain pushes until the vision pulls." I returned to my vision and began to see how the way I was living my life was out of alignment with that vision. I began to get really honest with myself. I knew I needed to step back, come into my body, and reclaim my feminine essence if I intended to continue.

I reclaimed the sacred morning time, began to eat organic and mostly raw food again, do yoga, and walk in the park with no headset. I could hear the birds again. I took the time for friends and just sitting on my deck overlooking the water.

I am a woman. It hurts me to push too hard. I have tremendous drive, and I am a woman. I need to have moments of intimacy, connection, pleasure, and just being. I need to be touched. Life needs to be juicy for me if I am to enjoy genuine prosperity.

I can balance these out with times of great focus and productivity. When I am in balance, honoring both the masculine and feminine aspects of me, my actions are then inspired and come from an expanded place of open-heartedness.

ENTER THE GODDESS LAKSHMI

One day when I was in the midst of reclaiming my true essence, the Hindu Goddess Lakshmi appeared to me. Yes, you heard it: She appeared on my computer. I was googling something, and there she was. She knew where to find me!

I knew her as the Goddess of Abundance and have since come to know her as so much more than that. She is the Goddess of Genuine Prosperity. The Hindu sacred texts, the Vedas, call her "the one who has the object and aim of uplifting mankind." Lakshmi is the embodiment of love, from which devotion to God flows. She also embodies material and spiritual prosperity, light, wisdom, fortune, fertility, generosity, courage, grace, beauty, and charm. She is said to bring good luck and to protect her devotees from all kinds of misery and money-related sorrows.

Tuning into the gracious energy of Lakshmi, I realized that it was this very energy that I needed to bring to my business. I saw how the pain of being disconnected from my feminine essence and the healing that came from returning to who I really am was the great lesson to be learned. I immediately began to attract the people I wanted to work with and to make the money that had been out of reach when I had been pushing too hard. I saw how I was meant to teach this to others.

This is true for all of us. Our great brilliance comes from removing what is not us so that who we are can brightly shine.

I shifted out of fear and began to experience the spiritual and financial prosperity that is my true nature—in an embodied way that included my emotions and sexuality, not just my mind—and the results were miraculous. By making the inner shift, even before the outer circumstances of my life changed, I opened the portal to prosperity. My income dramatically increased immediately, along with the joy I have when I am connected to my essence.

WE ALL FORGET WHO WE REALLY ARE

Scientists have been able to prove that everything is actually light alternating in particle and wave form, which is energy. Everything is energy: spirals and waves of energy.

When we take human birth, the vast light/energy of all that is becomes individualized in us. By taking birth, we lose the memory of how grand and magnificent we truly are. We come into the form of a human baby, and we are left seeking a mirror to remember who we are.

Since we came from within the source of all that is, the only true mirror of who we are is the source itself, which is also infinite abundance, which is love itself. It is so important to fully take that in: We are made of love itself, infinite in its abundance. We are each the individualized expression of the light of love in human 3-D form.

But as an infant, the first mirrors we encounter are usually Mom and Dad, which initiates the habit of looking outside of ourselves to know who we are. Since Mom and Dad have also been searching for who they are, they can only reflect back from their own limited sense of love and power, which is the legacy from their parents. Depending upon how well our parents reflect back who we really are, we are all left with some questions about our lovability, competence, worthiness, and other forms of self-doubt that continue to show up in our lives until we face the truth about them. With the help of our parents, we create a template, which leads us to unconsciously seek similar mirrors in our close relationships and in our business.

THE SACRED WOUND

The truth is that we all get wounded. I call this the sacred wound. I believe our soul determines how we will get wounded before we are even born because there is a beautiful sacred gift associated with that wound, which we are meant to discover.

We all adapt in some way to survive being wounded. That adaptation is a cover-up, or defense, against the feelings of being hurt. In covering up the hurt, we also cover up the gift. Really take that in. You are wired to recreate the stuff of your childhood in your life and business. This is the cause of relationship addictions and struggles, financial struggles, and the great disappointment you inevitably experience when you expect to fill your emptiness through someone or something else, including a business, before you have done the essential work of remembering who you really are.

This can show up in many ways in our business, from hiring people who cannot be trusted to trying to do it all yourself. It can be expressed through pushing too hard, procrastinating, charging too little, and engaging in countless forms of self-sabotage that recreate the pain of the past. These are all forms of fear (false evidence appearing real) that you must face when you decide to create a soul-centered business.

From a soul perspective, this is good news. You now get to take back the power you have given those lies in the first place. You get to create a new template based on the truth of who you are now.

From a human perspective, this can be really challenging and painful and can even lead you to be one of the majority who quit before they reap their heart's desire because you cannot successfully (joyfully and profitably) sustain something that does not feed your soul.

YOUR MINDSET MATTERS MOST

In truth, you can learn to shift out of fear and into love quickly if you have a tool that can remind you what is real and true in any given moment, no matter what is happening. This 3-step process, called SOS, can be used anytime you find yourself slipping into the unconscious mindset of limiting beliefs. You use it to remind yourself in a matter of seconds that you are co-creating your life, moment to moment, with the source of all creation. It can return you to a sense of calm and clarity quickly and keep you on track as you move through your day.

Step 1: Stop and tell yourself the story.

Whenever you are struggling, you have a story. You are the protagonist, and something seems to be the antagonist. Let's say you want to raise your rates and keep saying you will, yet months go by and you never do. Intellectually you know what you offer is worth more than what you are asking, but you have this story: People won't pay, the economy is so bad, I am already charging more than so and so...you know the drill.

So now, instead of these thoughts and feelings swirling around, you write the story down. If you are struggling, you have created this drama (the ego loves drama). You are in the mindset of a victim, which is without power.

Step 2: Own it all. You have created it.

I love this step because I immediately feel a sense of personal power when I own it all. When you say, "Yes, I have created this situation where I am working too hard and resenting it," "I have created this situation where my client is dissatisfied," or "Yes, I have created this situation where I am feeling unfulfilled in my relationship," you put yourself back in the driver's seat of your life.

Step 3: Surrender.

This step is key and so very challenging for most people. Once you have owned things, the tendency is to try to solve the problem with your mind. If you could, you would not be struggling.

I asked some very high-powered entrepreneurs what their biggest obstacles are to being in the flow and accomplishing the countless tasks they must deal with every day. Here are some: perfectionism, the need to control, the inner gremlins constantly saying it is not good enough, leading them to push harder, not sleep enough, and fall into a sense of resignation.

Surrender is not resignation, but a conscious releasing of resistance and basically declaring to the universe "I can't do this alone." You are saying to a power far greater than your ego, "I surrender, and open myself to your guidance. I align with the source of all power." With this, I suggest you take several conscious breaths, dropping your shoulders, feeling the burden being lifted.

S   **Story**

O   **Own it all**

S   **Surrender**

You can do it quickly, no matter where you are. Your affirmations will have more power because you have released the resistance you have to the moment.

The spiritual teacher Byron Katie says that, without our stories, we are pure love and, when we argue with reality, we only lose 100% of the time. When you own and surrender your story, you return to the undercurrent of love that is always present. You accept what is.

The result is that the actions you take are infused with the power of your soul, rather than of your ego, and you begin to attract the people and situations that support you to claim your very unique significance in the grand scheme of things. You realize that all of creation is designed to support your highest expression of yourself; the more your energy is a match for the vision you hold, the more gracefully and purposefully you manifest the life you deeply desire.

Kuumba Nia

Kuumba Nia, "The Me Mastery Mentor," works with heart-centered business owners to create and grow successful businesses from a place of self-knowledge and self-mastery. Known for blending the principles of authentic leadership, universal law, and energy-alignment tools, Kuumba delivers simple ways for entrepreneurs to reignite the passion for their business so they can step up to the challenges they face or step out into something new. Kuumba is the author of *The Circle of One: How to Heal Your Relationships and Live Your Truth.*

www.kuumbana.com

www.facebook.com/kuumba.nia

www.facebook.com/pages/Kuumba-Nia/ 132261106868517?sk=app_243527475679891

https://twitter.com/kuumbania10

http://uk.linkedin.com/in/kuumbania

· ·

Kuumba is one of these women who, when they start speaking as in "walking in" any space, you can do nothing but notice their presence. She is as authentic as it can get and is a real creator of her own destiny.

Thanks, Kuumba, for sharing a glimpse of your great expertise with me and all the women who will enjoy your chapter.

{ LESSON 25 }

BUILDING YOUR BUSINESS
FROM THE CIRCLE OF ONE

by Kuumba Nia

. . . .

A few years ago, I developed a tool to help my clients work through some of the blocks that they were facing when trying to show up authentically in their lives. Many of them were heart-centered, spiritual women who were constantly feeling the tug of being in relationships, running their businesses, or carrying out a role in their job that was completely at odds with what they felt and how they wanted to be in the world. Points of view and opinions taken on from family, friends, and colleagues had left them in a constant battle with what was true for them and the ways they were told that they ought to behave in life, love, and business. Often, they had no idea that it was this dichotomy that was leaving them unhappy and unfulfilled. They just knew that they were.

And so the Circle of One was born.

The tool itself is a simple step-by-step process based on an even simpler premise: In life, everyone and everything around you reflects a facet of you. Things, people, events, and circumstances gather to form metaphorical mirrors that continuously show us ourselves and provide clues that let us know how we're showing up in the world. I call this process "stepping into the Circle of One" because ultimately it's all about you. You are the starting and end point in all events in your life and, consequently, are compelled to look closely at your part in everything.

Despite its lack of complexity, I have found it to be one of the most powerful and effective means of guaranteeing continual personal growth, spiritual expansion, and personal success.

What do I mean by success? Well, for each of us, the answer's different. Only you can know what it means for you. For me, it's what Neale Donald Walsch refers to as creating "the grandest version of the greatest vision of who you really are." It's about being whole, being liberated, and stepping into my "Godself."

So how do you create this "great vision"? Well, I guess it's by truly knowing yourself, telling the truth of who you really are, and committing to take the action that will guarantee your growth and expansion.

Yes, I know. I make it sound so simple, and for the most part, it is. What it is not is easy. Why? Because the greatest obstacle to all of this is our lack of self-awareness, our inability to clearly see how we're showing up in the world so that we can use that knowledge to become the truly wondrous and wonderful beings that we were put on this planet to be.

When you embrace the underpinning principles of the Circle of One and step into the circle with a sense of connection, self-responsibility, personal empowerment, honesty, trust, self-awareness, and commitment to action, you cannot help but see your thoughts, beliefs, and behaviors reflected back to you through the ever-unfolding events around you. As if by magic, you start to see what's really going on.

If you're surrounded by dishonest people, then there is somewhere in your life that you are being dishonest. Similarly, if you find yourself in conflict with others, then there is somewhere in your life that you are in conflict. Through the circle, you get to see just how truthful you are being with others and whether what you say is congruent with what you do; most importantly, you get the chance to change it.

So how can the Circle of One help you build your business?

First and foremost, it will give you the knowledge of self, and with it, the gift of your personal power; the power to be, do and have anything you choose from a place of self mastery.

It's worth remembering that who you are being in your personal life has an immediate and direct impact on the results in your business. Someone once told me that "how you do anything is how you do everything." The truth is, we are our business, and the way we show up in life is the same way we show up there.

So if there is something that is showing up in your personal life that is keeping you stuck or unable to grow in the way you desire, you can almost guarantee that aspects of that same issue will come around in your business. Although you might be happy to dodge the consequences of this in your personal life, you can only do that for so long in your business.

Although the Circle of One was initially designed as a personal development tool to help guide people through their everyday relationships, it has increasingly proved itself to be even more useful in helping business owners examine and understand the dynamics they create in their business through their relationships with themselves, their team, and their clients.

Take Vanessa for example. When I started working with Vanessa, she had a small accounting firm that was doing well in terms of the number of clients it serviced, but as far as managing the workload was concerned, Vanessa and her team were seriously struggling on all fronts. They were overwhelmed, under-skilled, and over-reliant on Vanessa to give direction and make decisions that could have easily been handled by the team. Her clients often didn't pay on time, and Vanessa complained that they tried to "nickel and dime" her on every invoice. The situation had left Vanessa exhausted, stressed, and resentful of the work that she had once loved.

When we completed her circle, it became glaringly obvious why Vanessa was experiencing these specific challenges in her business. Having identified the particular traits that were manifesting in her staff and clients, I asked her "where in your business are you being overly reliant on others, not trusting your own judgment, and penny pinching on your most important purchases?"

It became clear to Vanessa at once. She had continually delayed her purchase of a crucial piece of software for the business. Although she knew that its installation would transform the way her business ran, freeing up time for her and doubling productivity, she had stalled in the hopes that the price would go down. It hadn't.

Similarly, in an effort to cut corners on salary costs, Vanessa had employed people who were willing, but unable to do the job required. They did not have the skills or qualifications; consequently, Vanessa had to oversee their every move. The truth was that deep down, she didn't really believe that she could attract the caliber of staff that her business required.

Upon closer inspection, we could see that precisely the things that Vanessa had complained of in others she had been doing herself. The shift in energy was almost palpable as Vanessa realized what had been going on. She stopped judging herself and allowed herself to fully receive the wave of compassion that she felt for what had been her long and lonely struggle.

Together, we worked out an action plan, and Vanessa immediately scheduled the purchase of the software package and began the process of recruiting suitably qualified staff and handing over responsibility to the team. Not only had she begun the challenge of trusting them, but she had begun trusting in herself and her ability to run her business from a point of expansion and not contraction.

The insight gained from using the Circle of One as a reference point with this client—and many others—has been invaluable, enabling them to see themselves for who they really are and to act in honor of that.

Building your business from the Circle of One is the key to your success. It allows you to choose the kind of business owner you wish to be in this and every moment, no matter what the context. It helps you to get clear about what you stand for and why. It requires you to be honest about who you are and how you're being in all your relationships, all of the time.

Most importantly, it's about taking that awareness and allowing it to guide you in growing yourself and building your business. Why not step into the circle?

So now it's your turn. Let me invite you into the Circle of One to try this exercise.

1. Take a piece of paper and a pen and draw a circle in the center of the page. Write your name in the middle of it.

2. Draw three "spider legs" coming out from the circle spaced out as if the circle were covering a Y.

3. Think of 3 people in your business or organization that irritate, annoy, anger, or challenge you and write their names at the end of each "spider leg."

4. Go around the circle, and for each named person, list 3 or 4 of their negative traits or characteristics that stand out the most for you.

5. Then go around the circle again, highlighting the commonalities.

6. List those common traits separately, then ask yourself "where in my life am I being that way?"

7. Ask yourself "what is required to move on?"

8. Take the necessary action.

A full explanation of the process and underpinning principles can be found in *The Circle of One: How to Heal Your Relationships and Live Your Truth*:

(http://www.kuumbania.com/resources/the-circle-of-one/).

Ana Lucia Novak

Ana Lucia Novak is a social media strategist, technical trainer, speaker and co-author of *Making Your Connections Count* (Thrive Publishing, 2011). Ana Lucia delivers big-company social media savvy to entrepreneurs; her role as a social media manager, coach, and advisor helps individuals and businesses embrace social media marketing as an extension to their brand, with a detailed blueprint for building a streamlined and seamless platform to generate SEO and online traction as well as attract and build trusting relationships through effective content marketing, including blogging and video. Ana Lucia offers Do It Yourself, Do It With You, and Do It As You social media programs for small businesses and start-ups.

 http://www.Facebook.com/AnaSocialMarketing

 http://www.Twitter.com/AnaLuciaNovak

 http://www.Linkedin.com/in/AnaLuciaNovak

 http://www.Pinterest.com/AnaLuciaNovak

Although I haven't got the chance to meet Ana Lucia personally, I have to admit I'm a fan. Twitter is still a big mystery to me, and I know it might also be for some of you. I couldn't leave that topic out of the book; to do so would be unthinkable. So it was clear I needed to find the pearl who was walking her talk.... Have you checked how many followers Ana Lucia has?

Thanks, Ana Lucia, for being part of this project. You belong in this book, and your chapter speaks for your expertise in a major way.

{ LESSON 26 }

A WHOLE NEW WORLD—LEARN WHY YOU NEED TWITTER

by Ana Lucia Novak

. . . .

Twitter has been around since 2006 and has more than half a billion registered profiles. Clearly Twitter is an active platform that streams news, education, photos, videos, and comments about every topic imagined 24 hours, 7 days per week—and all within 140 characters. Twitter is a wonderful channel to share your products and services as well as meet new prospects who don't know that they need you until they meet you online.

Twitter is still new to some people, as most aren't sure how to implement Twitter as a communication channel for them or for their business. Twitter also seems to be overwhelming and hard to learn. Some people think that Twitter is a waste of precious time and immediately dismiss the idea of using Twitter for business. Although I've been using Twitter since 2008, I want you to know it wasn't love at first sight! I resisted Twitter for several years because I simply did not have time to "chat with strangers about mundane things" and thought it was a tool for kids.

I changed my mind about Twitter after reading an online news article about a young American male who had been tweeting from a prison cell in another country and how the U.S. government managed to get him out and back on American soil. The story tugged at my heart and triggered my curiosity to finally check out Twitter. I realized that if Twitter has value for an individual, imagine how Twitter can help your business grow? Here are the latest statistics about Twitter:

- Since the dawn of Twitter, there have been a total of 163 billion tweets, and 175 million tweets were sent from Twitter every day in 2012. Interestingly, Twitter now has more than half a billion registered profiles, with more than 140 million in the U.S. alone. During some special occasions and events, Twitter generates tens of thousands of tweets every second. The average Twitter user has tweeted 307 times.

- Interestingly, 56% of customer tweets to companies are being ignored. It's said that 50% of the consumers give a brand a week of time to reply to their question before they stop doing business with them. In addition, 86% of consumers tend to pay more for a better customer experience while 82% of them stopped doing business with a company because of poor customer experience.

- It seems friends' suggestions work here too, as friends suggest 69% of follows on Twitter itself. Indeed, 26% of retweets are provoked by a request to retweet.

Source: http://www.dazeinfo.com/2013/01/10/social-media-statistics-2013-facts-figures-facebook-twitter/#ixzz2JnK8fGX9

If you haven't been sold on Twitter yet, I encourage you to read this chapter and experiment with Twitter. Your competitors are on Twitter, and so are your potential customers.

- Twitter is a valuable tool—consider it as an extension of you, your online presence, and a bridge that connects you to potential customers, partners, and new friends.

- Twitter also provides instant access to the world, where you can communicate your knowledge and expertise by posting your content, your favorite quotes, and videos.

- You can use Twitter to share upcoming teleseminars, webcasts, your eBooks, training, and coaching programs, thereby growing your email list and client base.

- You can set up listening streams to listen to what others are saying about you and your competitors as well as listen for opportunities for new business partnerships, a speaking gig, or a chance to co-author a book.

- There are a number of tools that make Twitter manageable, so you can spend quality time engaging online while generating traction toward your online presence.

Twitter is a resourceful platform, and the proof is in the numbers; it's people that have made Twitter valuable, otherwise this chapter wouldn't be here for you to read.

I have found Twitter to drive traffic to my website, increase webinar registrations, attract ideal clients, and shorten my learning curve on many topics. Twitter has afforded me rich connections worldwide and opened doors to opportunities that I would have missed had I not been on Twitter. Are you ready to take a leap of faith and leverage this powerful online channel?

Here are some basic best practices to get you started:

Create a profile: Use your first and last name; if it's not available, use your business name and continue the process of creating a profile on Twitter. Enter your full name, location, and website URL as well as add optimized keyword descriptions in the bio section. Your bio section is where you should enter a mix of who you are as a person, what you offer, and something personal about you. If you are unsure as to how to describe yourself, check out a few people's profiles or conduct a quick search within Twitter (using the search bar) to see how others identify themselves. This should give you some ideas as to how to craft your personal bio and inject your personality. Having an optimized set of keyword descriptions will help you get found within the Twitter search as well as in Twitter directories.

To Facebook or Not: You have the option of connecting your Facebook profile or page. I don't recommend that you do this until you have mastered Twitter and have a solid strategy in place. If you have not opened up your personal Facebook profile to acquaintances and potential customers, you may not want Tweets feeding your Facebook newsfeed, which will overwhelm your family and friends.

Upload Your Headshot or Logo: If you named your Twitter handle by your company name, upload your logo or a professional headshot if you are the CEO or founder of your company.

Twitter-branded Page: Decide what background you would like to have in your banner (behind your headshot). You might want to hire a designer to create a banner and a Twitter-branded page. You can have it done professionally for $99.00 or visit Fiverr.com to find a designer who would be happy to do it for a very low price.

Find Followers: Twitter isn't about the quantity of followers, but seeking and following ideal followers who you can engage with on a regular basis. You can find followers by linking/syncing your Twitter profile with your address or by keywords within the Twitter search bar and from Twitter directories.

Create Twitter Lists. I use lists to organize and manage the growth of my Twitter community. Create a list based on a theme or category and as you follow people back, file them under the appropriate category so you can manage your Twitter followers' conversations. The beauty of these lists is that you can create up to 20 lists and file 500 people per list. People can subscribe to your lists, and you can subscribe to other people's lists. Often you will learn that your Twitter profile has been added to a list. It's quite a compliment to have your profile listed on someone's list. The Hootsuite application and the iPad/iPhone apps make it easy to view and engage from your lists

Once your profile is complete, I suggest exploring the following tools:

REPUTATION MANAGEMENT TOOLS

Sync your Twitter profile to Kred.com, Klout.com, and PeerIndex.com.

CURATE CONTENT AND PUBLISH REAL TIME TO TWITTER

People follow you because of how you add value to their lives, usually through your content. If you can't write enough blogs, then mix it up with other people's content. Remember to find content that educates, entertains, adds value, informs, and shortens their learning cycle! Here are a few tips:

- Find content on Alltop.com or Technorati, or use Google to conduct a search around a keyword or topic.

- After reviewing blogs or content that complement your business, gather a list of RSS feeds. It should look like this one: **http://feeds.feedburner.com/socialana/Analucia**

- Use a tool like Dlvr.it and set up this tool with your favorite RSS feeds from various resources. Dlvr.it allows you set up different feeds for different platforms, so you can set up your own blog RSS feed to update your LinkedIn status while setting up relevant and mixed content into Twitter. Dlvr.it also allows you to send content to Google+.

- You can also set up automated content using Hootsuite's RSS feed tool, but I prefer Dlvr.it because you are able to append hashtags at the end of the headline as well as select a preferred day of the week and time to post fresh content to your social channels.

SET UP HOOTSUITE AS YOUR SOCIAL MEDIA MANAGEMENT DASHBOARD:

Hootsuite is by far one of the best social media management dashboards. It helps you manage your time, curate and publish content, schedule posts, monitor feeds, lists, and keywords, and measure Google Analytics and Facebook Insights. Once you get oriented to this tool, you will find that it is easy to use each day. Hootsuite also has a few applications that will help you find assorted content that you can post or schedule using Hootsuite's scheduler tool. Hootsuite allows you to integrate Twitter, Twitter lists, Facebook profiles, Facebook pages, LinkedIn profile and groups, YouTube, Instagram, and more.

TWITTER DIRECTORIES:

After you organize your Twitter with appropriate lists, you can submit your profile to several directories. These directories are rich in terms of seeking and targeting ideal quality followers (with the exception of WeFollow) as well as being found by people who are searching for your products and services. Hence, containing a proper keyword description in your Twitter profile is important in order for you to get found online.

- **Twellow** is a large database and a valuable tool. Create a profile first. Twellow will pull up people they suggest you follow (based on the keywords of your profile, so make sure your Twitter profile has distinct keywords). Submit your profile to 10 categories. Search for people by location, industry, and/or titles. This is a great tool for local business (restaurants, spas, doctors, dentists) to add local followers and then use Twitter and Foursquare to communicate specials, offers, etc. Complete the advanced profile section—take advantage of the real estate here, enter keyword descriptions of your business, services, and your brand. Include all your social profiles.

- **WeFollow**—here you add your Twitter profile to "categories or tag words." Be careful though; a word like "coach" could pull in sports, teams, or sports coach into your Twitter followers section, so be explicit in your keywords.

- **TweetFind**—here you can submit your business, and it's worth paying for the upgrade $9.95 per year.

- **Listorious**—submit your profile and lists. This is a great platform to seek/target quality followers and a great platform to follow other people's lists by categories or topics.

- **Twibs**—submit your business and up to 4 keywords, blog URL, and product page URL. It's a directory, and I encourage you to explore the additional tabs.

As you can see, Twitter can be used as a business development tool to grow your business and foster relationships, but it's important to know the proper protocols on Twitter so that you make a good first impression, not turn off your followers and ruin relationship opportunities.

TWITTER SUCCESS TIPS:

- Keep your tweets succinct. According to BuddyMedia, tweets that contained fewer than 100 characters received 17% higher engagement than longer tweets.

- According to BuddyMedia, Tweeting during the day is the way to go. Tweets during "busy hours" (8 a.m. to 7 p.m.) receive 30% higher engagement than tweets published outside that time frame. This includes tweets published on Saturday and Sunday.

- Use 1 or 2 trending hashtags. Studies have shown that Tweets with hashtags received two times more engagement than those without them, but limit the hashtags to two.

- It's okay to ask your followers to retweet (all spelled out). According to BuddyMedia, tweets that contain the words "RT" or "Retweet" receive 12 times more retweet shares compared to those that don't include a call to action.

- Use images in your tweets. According to the BuddyMedia research, tweets that contained pictures or links to images received twice the engagement.

Source: http://www.buddymedia.com/newsroom/2012/06/buddy-media-twitter-tweeting-best-practices/

Show up daily and greet your followers; read content from the feeds or from Twitter lists; comment and retweet; acknowledge mentions and thank people who retweet you. Use Follow Friday tools to sort your Twitter followers and help you mention your followers to your community. Find and share content that interests you and your community, answer questions, and share tools and cheat sheets (yours and other people). Be kind, share funny photos and videos, and basically just be real.

THOU SHALL NOT:

Steal other people's tweets

Spam your followers

Slander, harass, lie, and / or gossip about anyone, whether true or false

Be one-sided

Be idle

The key to success on Twitter is to show up daily and to be known as the "go-to" person for your industry or niche. Even if you spend 15 minutes per day, there is no limitation to how you can use Twitter for business. When you practice the PCP method—persistency, consistency, patience—you will develop your own style, voice, and rich connections that will make you look forward to visiting Twitter. Continue to develop smart strategies, leverage tools, and apply tactics. Don't be afraid to think outside the box and try different forms of content. Make it your mission to make the message about them (your community). Doing so will enhance your online presence and send tons of traffic to your website while growing a rich community of friends, potential partners, authors, speakers, and thought leaders.

Kat Mikic

Kat is passionate about helping passionate people. She's the director of Women's Web Marketing and also the *Zen Wellness Magazine*. Kat is a social media veteran who teaches women how to combine their passion with a desire in the marketplace to grow a global business and online presence. She can show you how to combine the internet, social media, and video to create a global brand and business that can make you money in your sleep.

http://womenswebmarketing.com

• •

Kat is from Australia and, once again, I got to meet her through Facebook. (By the way, are you convinced now that Facebook is a useful tool?) Pleasantries aside, Kat contacted me a few months ago with her story and I have to admit I automatically listed her in my "future JV pool." I knew there was more than what met the eye in her experience. As you'll read in the following pages, I was right!

Thank you, Kat, for playing the game of a world adventure with me. You have a gift—don't bury it.

A WOMAN OF INFLUENCE—HOW TO RISE TO SUCCESS WITH SOCIAL MEDIA AND VIDEO MARKETING

by Kat Mikic

When I was a little girl I remember looking with admiration at kids who had loving parents, nice cars, fancy homes, and nice clothes. I on the other hand had an abusive alcoholic father, rode in a car that looked like an army tank, and frequently wore second-hand clothes from my cousins. I felt like a complete alien. I was 10 years old when I decided that my life was going to be different. I started my first job delivering papers the next year and have earned an income ever since.

To be honest, the sheer fact that I am where I am today is my version of a modern-day miracle. I come from a place of low confidence and poor self-esteem, which led to many unsavory choices throughout my teenage years—at one point leading me to the top of a bridge, where I went with the intention of jumping off and ending it all. The only thing that stopped me was the thought of my mum being told that I was gone. I know it sounds crazy, but I felt like I had an angel with me, telling me that I had too much to do here. So I ran to the other side of the bridge with a steely determination in my gut, deciding that it was now my mission to help other girls who had come from my kind of situation. I didn't know the what or the how, but it turns out that here I am and that's what I do every day. Pretty cool, hey!

By the age of 28, I had a partnership in a thriving tourism business, my own business "on the side," a property portfolio, and a baby on the way. I thought I had it all. By the time my daughter had arrived, my relationship had failed, my dad had died, and it was pretty much the start to losing everything. After the birth of Jessee, I re-launched online, but I had to do it on a shoestring budget because I was going broke and desperately had to turn it all around.

The realization that came later was The Woman of Influence—a greater mission that was to educate women to put a "back end" in to their business and have alternative income streams so that they could stand strong independent of a man and of having to trade time for money. Most women believe they're independent, but when seriously looking into their finances, they realize that if they were forced to go it on their own income, they would struggle—especially if they are relying on trading time for money.

It was my struggle that inspired my future. At the depths of my misery, my 8-month-old babe in my arms, I gathered up everything I knew about online marketing and social media and launched Women's Web Marketing, investing just $250 with a return of $1,000 in my sleep within the first 2 weeks of launch (in my sleep!). It was nuts! I did the work once and created the potential to get paid over and over again. It was this that ultimately established the beginnings of the Woman of Influence program—I just didn't quite know it!

When I decided to launch the *Zen Wellness Magazine*, I once again did this with a minimal outlay. In fact, this time I didn't spend a cent. Within 24 hours of deciding to launch, I had built my own website, generated more than 100 fans on my fanpage, had 20 contributors ask to be a part of it, and had 3 requests for advertising!

Generating interest in what you do, people asking to work with you instead of you chasing them, and closing sales will all become easy when you have this complete recipe in place.

This is the power of being a Woman of Influence.

Finding clients and making money will no longer be a problem. In fact, on the morning of writing this chapter I received a phone call from a lady who said in her opening sentence, "Hi Kat, I am in your group—

congrats on that. I love what you do, and I have been watching your videos and reading your posts and now I have a problem and I know you can help me."

I am not sharing my story of the past to impress you, but merely to impress upon you that if I can do this, then so can you. The road has not been easy, but in truth, I now understand that, for me to arrive at this destination and to really truly be able to help women make a real impact on the world, I needed to experience what it was like to come from a place of little to no self-esteem, self-loathing, self-doubt, self-sabotage—the dregs of ugliness.

What is it you want to do? What ignites your soul, takes your breath away, and makes you want to stand at the top of a mountain screaming "hell freaking yes!"? What makes you come so absolutely alive that you are infectious?! It is that—that very thing that you can share with the world! So what's stopping you?

It's incredible just how many amazing, seemingly confident women I meet who are doing amazing things yet completely choke when it comes to "getting out there" in front of the world on a massive scale.

My chapter is all about launching your business using social media and video marketing. We are so fortunate to be blessed with the internet and social media—it is so easy for an ordinary Jane to start building an online profile. And guess what? It doesn't have to be perfect, you just have to get it going.

So then, what does it mean to be a Woman of Influence?

A Woman of Influence is a strong, talented, fearless woman who is on a mission to use her innate gifts and talents to make a difference in the lives of others and maybe even a massive impact on the world. She knows she is here on Earth to achieve great things!

First, what you have to understand is that there is a strategy behind this—a method, if you like. But the main key ingredient is you: Be yourself! Intertwine it with this ingredient list.

INGREDIENT LIST

1. A well-thought-out personal brand, which can be intertwined with a business entity (as I have chosen).

2. A mission—what is it that you love? What are you putting out there?

3. An audience—who wants/needs what you have?

4. Photography and a logo that represent you.

5. A website designed to back up your movement.

6. A compelling bio throughout all of your social media channels.

7. An end in mind—where do you want to lead your audience (important for money making because you work back from here)?

8. A way to accept money (e.g., PayPal).

9. An enticing offer.

10. Value—things that you can give away that re-enforce that you know what you know. Offer massive value wherever you can.

11. Networks—strong networks with influencers, tribes, and supporters.

THE TOOLS

-   WordPress website; designed to be social and engage with your followers, capture visitors, build a tribe, and make sales

-   Well-developed Facebook profile with Facebook fan page interlinked to personal profile

-   YouTube account

-   Twitter account

-   LinkedIn profile

-   Pinterest profile

The Woman of Influence method is all about you being your true, authentic self and being present.

Nothing communicates better with your audience than video. Bringing video marketing into your overall marketing strategy will allow you to build rapport and connect with a wider scope of people.

- Videos get listed in Google searches.

- Video helps people feel like they know you.

- Video has the ability to break down the pre-sales barrier

- Video can be used for instruction and for sales.

- The minute you take the mic, people will start to perceive you as an expert.

Making videos can be overwhelming at first. People wonder what to talk about and also who would care to listen. Trust me, there are people who want to know what you have to share; you just have to understand how to find them. Figure out the who, what, and where and then share your videos with them.

When you are ready to launch your business, put a video on your website. It's like you being there to greet your visitors without you actually being there—it's the very first point of leverage! Don't stress about getting it all right, just get it started and perfect as you proceed. Gather feedback and judge the response of your marketing campaigns, then adjust to address the feedback.

My heart is with you on this next step! Good luck beautiful Women of Influence!

See you on YouTube!

Katrin Faensen

Katrin Faensen, born in 1974 in Berlin, Germany, is an entrepreneur and change facilitator. She studied language, religion sciences, and social work in Erlangen and Berlin. She further qualified as social therapist and business coach focused on organizational development. Katrin worked as a manager in social institutions before she founded her own business and specialized as a change facilitator for companies. As an early digital native and high achiever, she lives the paradigm shift and walks her talk about understanding complexity and diversity.

✉ **katrinfaensen@the-virus.org**

www.selbst-wirksam.de (German)

www.the-virus.org

www.change-the-world-company

🐦 **@katrinfaensen/@changetheworldc/@virus_tweets**

in **http://de.linkedin.com/pub/katrin-faensen/44/b13/775**

🅦 **https://katrinfaensen.wordpress.com (German)**

. . . .

When I contacted Katrin to invite her to participate in this project, I had no idea she was about to deliver her third baby boy. Then, as the universe likes to conspire for our greatest good, I was glad to welcome her on the last day of the project after one of the other ladies had to drop out. The universe wanted Katrin to be in, and here she is. So Katrin wrote her chapter in just 2 little days, ensuring I got it on time to send to the editor. What a story, huh?

Thank you, Katrin, for jumping into the open seat and thank you to your husband, who took care of the baby to give you the time and space to write this fabulous chapter.

191

{ LESSON 28 }

TEARING DOWN THE WALLS—
THE ROAD TO INNOVATION
by Katrin Faensen

. . . .

*"The nature quality and the amount of change that you
want to see in the world is directly relative to the amount of
change that you are ready to go through inside yourself."
~Tim Merry, Teacher of the Chaordic Stepping Stones*

This chapter is about innovation. I don´t think it's necessary to go into too much detail about why it is important to be innovative these days. Look around. The world is changing, and it is changing fast. Ideas and news spread, power is distributed differently, and knowledge about today's challenges and possible solutions is available everywhere. We encounter a paradigm shift towards uncertainty, diversity, and collaboration instead of fixed rules, process standardization, and competition. Values change. These facts require that we change our ways of perceiving, thinking, feeling, organizing, and acting completely and regularly to stay relevant and successful. For me, this means being innovative. Innovation also means that renewal has to take place inside of us before it is possible on the outside.

In the next several pages, I will guide you through the concept of my business, theVirus, to explain how we are innovative and how we help others to be innovative. I will point out the necessary next steps on the road to innovation, and I will be honest about the difficulty of this undertaking in our daily lives. I will provide you with a lesson about the strange logic of what is to be done now and suggest an exercise you might find helpful while developing the skills to become innovative.

THEVIRUS: CHANGING THE WORLD ONE COMPANY AT A TIME

We're change facilitators at theVirus. We create viral cells in different countries and in different cities in the companies we work with. These cells inspire and infect for change. We strive to be contagious. We want to build a network of change-the-world-companies around the globe that can rely on each other. We remind you and your company of your dreams, values, and purposes. By asking the right questions, people wake up to what they really want to do. If asked in the right context and later allowed to live their truth and full potential within the company, employees become highly motivated, live up to their potential, and in the next step become innovative. They develop their own ideas and take responsibility for their actions. Such questions include:

- Why do you get up in the morning?

- Why do you really get up in the morning?

- What is your work here about?

- What is the most important thing you do for the company?

- Why do you do it?

- Why do you like it?

- Why is this important to you?

Humans are social beings. In the end what we do and want to do always relates to others. We are collaborative beings; we want to be recognized and helpful at the same time. We want to be meaningful and create sense. With such questions, it is possible to discover the personal values and purposes on the one hand and the most important things for the company on the other. With these data, the organization is able to become aware of itself through every staff member, realizing that he/she is part of something bigger, part of something that has common values and a shared purpose. The way to a relevant, innovative change-the-world-company is open because, consequently, people will try to create more meaning. By doing so, the company becomes relevant for its environment. Supporting open, transparent conversations with all the stakeholders ultimately leads to seriously healthy changes within the organism itself.

In this example, you can see quite well what it needs to develop innovation skills. We need to become aware that we are part of something bigger, find out why we do what we do, and be courageous to be curious and discover different points of view—to develop new ideas and purposes—to think out of the box. In the end, we have to dare to be outstanding.

Here is the big lesson on the path and my being honest about the difficulties: The most important question for realizing that we're all part of something bigger (thanks M. Marien for asking me the mother of all questions) is: How big is your perception of the concept of "we"? Do you mean the western society? Your family? Mankind? The universe and everything that's in it? Do you mean yourself, just you and all the bacteria, cells, and organic structures that create your organism and that you do not willingly control? Let me suggest that you ponder over this for a while. And let me come up with an assumption: As long as there is any group of people outside of your biggest we-concept that you're not able to include in your "we," it is not big enough to consequently shift paradigms.

If there is still a "they" to blame (bankers, drug dealers, neighbors, your mother-in-law), you're not taking full responsibility for your life. Innovation now means that you try to cross borders and tear down the walls between "them" and "us." Bad guys here, good guys there—it is so easy, but if we want to create a world in which trust and co-creation are the leading paradigms, we have to give up our binary concept of good and bad. We even have to give up our binary concept of you and me, mind and matter. Wake up and realize that I am many. This admittedly difficult mental leap is a powerful key to personal growth. You are many. Even the voices in your head arise from many different sources. It's not you who's talking, it's your parents, friends, teachers, the media, your spouse, your kids—and the combination, the essence of all this might be you.

Now, if we become aware that we're part of a bigger "we"—like the cells in our body are aware of us—we become able to change our point of view rapidly, leaving us capable of true understanding! Here lies one key to innovation: multi-perspectivity. Following this for a while, we become "commonable," able to collaborate at equal levels with others while appreciating all the participants in the game. This is one first approach to becoming innovative, and it is a lifelong issue. I regularly find myself pointing toward a "them" being responsible for any trouble in my life….

Here is the paradox: If the first step is to tear down the walls between "me" and "them" and to learn that "I" am no better than "you," the second step is to consciously rebuild walls of principles, to create a foundation you can stand on to become outstanding. This is about storytelling. Everything that happened to you leads to values and principles that you have and follow. It's the meaningful story of your life that you want to discover to become outstanding. We tend to look in awe at those great personalities we all know that were/are part of major changes for good on the planet, yet we dare not let our own lights shine. We intensely try to keep a low profile, we try not to attract too much attention, and in the same moment we complain that we do not reach our higher goals. So the task is to be a flexible part of the bigger picture and at the same time to be very clear about our principles and values while being totally authentic about who we are.

When I understood that my unique selling point (which makes me stand out) is shifting paradigms, I started daring to live up to my principles and values without compromise. We are allowed to speak our truth as clearly and loudly as we can and stick with it. At the same time, we need to be aware that our truth is just one of many; if we encounter something more meaningful, we are challenged to tear down the walls again and rebuild them within us on stronger values and principles. I call this "running a worldview update."

So how do we implement this into our daily practice? I had a teacher who opened the door for me to understanding the paradox of duality within oneness—that's what it is what we're talking about here. Feel free to adopt or change whatever suits you. My recommendation is that you sit down at least once a week. Take pen and paper and write down the situations you encountered that you did not understand.

Write down every two facts that you just can't bring together in a reasonable way. For example, how can it be that here in Germany it is night time and over there in Washington it is broad daylight? Or my partner says he loves me, but how can he then forget my birthday all the time? Then take some time to find the beliefs behind those problems that hinder you from understanding. Maybe your concept of earth as a disk needs to be reconsidered? The example with your partner is a stronger one. Check your and others' values and definitions of concepts like "love" and "birthday." Try to find the source belief that leads to your incomprehension. Write it down: "I believe that love means to think about each other at significant dates and be creative with presents." It is important that you do not judge. You are part of something bigger. Now try to find any one argument (even if it sounds weird) that fits into the gap and helps you see. Try to think as another person, leaving your beliefs aside for a while. The argument might be: Love to him means something completely different; besides, I never told him how important it is for me that he remembers my birthday. Write these bridging arguments down and keep them with you for the next week. Try to think this way at least once a day. Rethink your values and principles concerning these topics. Start with easy things and work your way to the real challenges (e.g., wars). How can a father of kids work at an arms manufacturer for landmines?

This exercise will help you see more clearly than ever before, and it will help you understand the problems/challenges we run across at the moment. It will also broaden your "we" concept and open your eyes to many different perspectives and ideas, thereby planting the most important seed for being innovative.

This is one part of our work with companies. One of the most pressing challenges for humans in our world today is our lack of understanding each other. Helping people within companies understand each other leads to better communication and is part of the way to become innovative as a company.

Terry Wildemann

For intuitive business alchemist and success coach Terry Wildemann, studying and understanding how to achieve success in business and life has been a passion and lifelong quest. She merges her extensive business experience with her holistic and Law of Attraction knowledge in her speaking, coaching, and professional development workshops to help entrepreneurs and professionals transform their businesses and lives. Terry's weekly Blog Talk Radio show, "Coffee With Terry: Where Business and Spirituality Meet", offers business building wisdom from both Terry and her guests. Listen in and join in the conversation at **www.coffeewithterry.com**. Even better, apply to be a guest!

http://www.HeartCenteredSuccess.com
http://www.CoffeeWithTerry.com

f http://Facebook.com/TerryWildemann

f http://Facebook.com/HeartCenteredSuccess

f http://Facebook.com/CoffeeWithTerry

f http://Facebook.com/CallofTheRose

🐦 http://Twitter.com/TerryWildemann

🐦 http://Twitter.com/CoffeeWithTerry

🐦 http://Twitter.com/CallofTheRose

📌 http://Pinterest.com/TerryWildemann

in http://LinkedIn.com/in/TerryWildemann

Terry is a bona fide Power House, she knows how to work with the Universe like nobody else. She inspires trust and gives out so much of herself. I was lucky enough to have the chance of being featured on her radio show 'Coffee with Terry' and it was pure bliss. She lives and breathes love.

Thank you, Terry, for being part of this book. I'm honored to be able to share your message with our audience.

{ LESSON 29 }

ATTRACT SUCCESS IN BUSINESS AND LIFE
by Terry Wildemann, CEC, CPCC

Do you ever wonder why some people seem to easily attract everything they want, yet others live in a constant state of lacking? What's up with that! Take a good look at how those who seem to have the "Midas Touch" act and behave. They radiate success, confidence, and abundance, and it explodes at you from their body language, words, attitudes, and behavior. Now take a look at those who constantly struggle. Note their words, body language, and behavior. Chances are that they are the exact opposite of those of the more successful people.

Abundance and prosperity touch us in five distinct areas of our lives: career, finances, spirituality, health, and relationships. In my travels teaching professional development workshops and coaching, I'm often asked by my audiences and clients "How can I get more of what I want and less of what I don't want in all areas of my life?" It's an interesting question because you are constantly attracting experiences based on your words, phrases, and—most importantly—your vibes. It's called the Law of Attraction.

The Law of Attraction does only one thing, and it does it extraordinarily well: It's a matchmaker! It works every second of every minute of every day, week, month, and year. It works 24/7, continuously matching our vibes. Take a look at your life right now. Are you living life as you want it to be?

Take out the instruction manual for the Law of Attraction and you'll notice three simple steps that we have all been working with since birth:

1. Identify your desires.

2. Give your desire attention.

3. Allow your desire to manifest.

These steps sound easy enough, yet each one has a very important role in the manifestation process. To make it more interesting, I'm inviting "Jessica" to demonstrate how these steps work by having her do two things we do all the time: conducting a Google search and going out for a meal. First, let's look at the Google Search:

Step 1.   Identify Desire: Jessica decides she needs information for a marketing project.

Step 2.   Give Attention: Jessica types specific words and phrases into Google.

Step 3.   Allow: Jessica sits back and Google obediently displays the matches to her search.

The Law of Attraction works exactly the same way! Now, let's see how Jessica works with the Law of Attraction in a restaurant:

Step 1.   Identify Desire: Jessica decides she's hungry and chooses to treat herself to dinner.

Step 2.   Give Attention: Jessica goes to her favorite Chinese restaurant. Once seated, she gives the waiter her order.

Step 3.   Allow: Jessica sits back with her green tea and waits for her dinner to arrive. She does nothing but enjoy the process.

Now you may be thinking to yourself, "Terry, this is just too easy!" Does the Law of Attraction really work this way? Well, it's a case of being so simple that it's hard until you learn to listen, trust, and believe. This process is the same whether it's attracting relationships, career opportunities, health, or other things and events.

Your Words + Your Thoughts + Your Vibrations = Your Results

Let's focus on the power of words. Which of the following questions ring true for you?

How often do I...

...say negative things?

...focus on what's wrong instead of what's right?

...criticize and judge others?

...read negative stuff in the newspapers and watch negative stuff on TV?

...play violent and negative video games?

...tell the world about all of my aches and pains?

...talk about not being able to afford things because I am broke?

Chances are if the above phrases resonate with you, you are experiencing these issues in your life. Is that what you really want? Holding up the mirror can be painful, but the results of looking in that mirror closely and changing those things that don't feel good can be transformational.

Let's begin the shift by closely examining the words and phrases that we commonly use:

Can't, Don't, Not, No

How many times a day do you say can't, don't, not, or no? We are masters at using these words. Since the Law of Attraction delivers what you focus on, it makes sense to actually say what you want instead of what you don't want. For example, if you say to someone "don't leave the door open", the Law of Attraction hears, "leave the door open"; thus, more of that will happen. What you want the person to do is "close the door". State what you want them to do instead. Make sense?

How do the phrases in both of the columns below affect you when reading them?

INSTEAD OF THIS...	SAY THIS...
I can't find a job. I'm unemployed.	I'm employable and can find a job I enjoy and that pays well.
I can't find a good relationship.	I can/will attract a great relationship that's full of trust and fun.
I can't lose weight.	I do healthy things to get my body fit every day.
I can't find the time to...	All the time I need will be available.
I can't get well.	I get healthier every day.
I can't pay for that.	The money will show up.
I can't do that.	I will do that and trust that what I need will appear.

How do these phrases feel to you? Is doubt filtering through your mind? It doesn't surprise me. Stick with me. You'll soon learn how to shift the doubt.

INSTEAD OF THIS...	SAY THIS...
Don't leave the door open.	Close the door.
Don't drive fast.	Drive safely.
Don't fail your test.	Ace your test.
Don't do that.	Do this.
I don't know what to do.	I want insights on what to do.
Don't touch that.	Leave that alone.

Don't park the car in the driveway.	Park the car in the street.
Don't cut my hair like this.	Cut my hair like this.
I don't want to be fat.	I want to be slim, trim, and healthy.
Don't buy that tight-fitting jacket.	Buy a jacket that fits well.
I am not doing it.	I am doing this.
No, I won't….	I will….
That cannot be happening!	That is happening!
No, I won't do that.	I can do this.
I'm not listening to this.	I am listening to ….
I don't want an expensive car.	I want a car that fits my budget.
No one is coming to my event.	The people who are meant to be here will be here.

RELEASING DOUBT

Now, you might be thinking to yourself that even though you shift away from constantly using can't, don't, not, and no, you are still doubting that this works. Let's add the powerful phrase "I'm in the process of…" to the beginning of the positive phrases and see if it makes a difference for you.

NEGATIVE PHRASES (don't want…)	POSITIVE PHRASES (what do I want?)
I don't like my body.	I'm in the process of liking my body.
I don't know how to do this.	I'm in the process of figuring this out.

I'm not feeling well.	I'm in the process of feeling better.
I'm fat.	All the time I need will be available.

Hmm, doesn't that feel better? Using the phrase "I'm in the process of…" eliminates the doubt and makes what you want feel truer for you! Now, try placing it before each of the positive phrases listed in the previous tables. I'm sure you'll notice a big difference. This phrase helps shift into the positive state of "allowing" in step three of the Law of Attraction by eliminating the self-sabotage that gets in the way of belief and trust.

CONTRAST SHEET EXERCISE

Now you know what to do to attract more of what you want and less of what you don't want by changing your words and phrases to shift your vibes! Use the following template to write your own phrases.

NEGATIVE PHRASES (What you don't want...)	POSITIVE PHRASES (Ask yourself, "So what do I want?)

Students have informed me that minimizing the use of the words can't, don't, not, and no in their writing improved the quality of their emails and documents because it forced them to rewrite and speak in a more positive manner, thereby creating positive experiences. Remember to add the "I am in the process of…" phrase to make it real for you. That simple phrase is golden!

AVOID NEGATIVITY

Shedding negativity in all areas of your life makes a huge difference! Focus on your life. There will be naysayers telling you that you can't do something. It happens to me all the time, and guess what? I have proven them wrong every time. It's quite liberating! The following suggestions will help keep you in the positive attraction mode.

- Stop talking about poor health; focus on attracting great health.
- Turn off negative TV; watch positive shows.
- Turn off negative talk radio; listen to positive talk radio.
- Turn off negative music; listen to positive music.
- Stop reading negative books and newspapers; diligently choose positive reading.

As you can see, the Law of Attraction is a very powerful law, and hopefully these suggestions will guide you on your path of attracting all of the positive things that you want in your life. To your success!

Christine Marmoy

Christine is a go-getter and a high-achieving woman. She thrives to courageously lead a global movement—a movement to inspire and empower women to collaborate in innovative ways to stand out from the crowd, be seen, and profit from their unique brilliance in the international marketplace. She is the founder of The Women's Edge Magazine, a publication designed by women for women. This magazine is a window into the world as it is currently distributed in 23 different countries.

www.coachingandsuccess.com
www.thewomensedgemag.com
www.christinemarmoy.com
www.successinhighheels.com

www.facebook.com/ChristineMarmoy

www.facebook.com/coachingandsuccess

www.facebook.com/TheWomensEdgeMag

@coachandsuccess

@WomensEdgeMag

{ LESSON 30 }

THERE ARE NO BORDERS TO A WOMAN'S POWER

by Christine Marmoy

. . . .

We live in a society where globalization is moving forward at an unstoppable pace. Businesses have been "going global" for decades now and no, don't worry, I'm not going to enter into the debate about whether or not it is, in reality, beneficial for all of us. However, what I can and want to highlight is how many women have remained stuck on the sidelines and missed their all-important seat on this business train!

I see it countless times: Women working only within certain geographical limits, as if venturing out any further would mean entering into unknown territory and, consequently, danger. Unfamiliar surroundings can be scary as they take you out of your comfort zone; however, this can also be a very satisfactory as well as challenging experience.

Some of my clients come to me so they can truly reach international status; they might want to become international speakers, offering their services outside their home country, entering into new markets, or teaching in other faraway lands. They understand that nowadays they cannot afford to impose any borders on their business. The world is becoming just one single big gathering place, and making your mark usually means having to do it on a worldwide level rather than just in your own city or even your own country.

I've been lucky. For a large part of my life, I held a position that required me to travel to many different places and to meet so many wonderful (as well as less great) people. As a result, I had to live in a lot of countries. Today, I can honestly say that it was a blessing. My daughter, who is 17 today, is so grateful for what this lifestyle has taught her, because that's something that cannot be gained just by sitting on the school bench!

We are very fortunate because we live in a time where borders are now virtually non-existent. Of course, you still need a passport and have to go through the sometimes uncomfortable formalities of customs, but if you travel at the speed of your fingertips, you are not bothered by any such formalities!

Today, you can go around the world without even leaving your computer—a major step forward that will shape the way countries will interact with each other for the future. Look what happened in Egypt during the civil "revolution": The government shut down the country, but they couldn't do it as fast as 140 characters on Twitter! The entire world knew what was going on there, live, as the powers that be made the mistake of underestimating what technology can and cannot do. This is just the beginning. No doubt more similar events will happen going forward.

Although technology encourages communication in various countries regardless of their geographical area, meeting people face to face is still the panacea of "no borders" when you look at it from a power point of view. Yet that is a domain where women are not always comfortable.

It's not enough anymore to think about doing business just in your community or even your country when globalization calls for a much wider marketplace. We've heard a lot of things about globalization, but remember that there is always an upside to every downside. However, what I see happening all too often is that women are left on the subs' bench in the global game. Unfortunately, most of the time they cling to that bench as if their life depended on it.

"I want to be an international speaker. I want to teach in other countries. I want to sell my programs throughout the world". This is what I hear day in and day out and it is absolutely brilliant. However, like anything else, you need to be prepared and plan for that, because on one level the rules can be the same, but on another level they are very different.

Human beings are human regardless of their country of origin. However, the way they communicate and the way they perceive the world is always different, and that is the very element you need to capture to ensure that your message is understood everywhere you are going to share it. Some specifics that you must embrace to be able to go global include:

- **Language:** Not everybody speaks English. If you want to enter a new market, you'll need to consider this point. There are, however, ways round this. One of my clients did a workshop in a non-English speaking country with the help of a translator. It was quite a fantastic experience for her, and her audience didn't miss out on any of her teaching.

- **Culture:** Yes, this aspect will make all the difference. You might not get your point across simply because your new audience doesn't connect with what you say or how you say it. They might need what you offer, but if you don't communicate in a way that will hit home, then it won't work.

- **Religion:** I don't really like to discuss religion because, for me, it is a matter for the heart and everybody is right in this respect. However, you'll need to take this aspect into account to make sure your business develops and thrives.

- **Tradition:** Tradition here is in terms of business. Every country or part of the world has its own particular way of conducting business, and you'll need to abide by these unwritten rules if you want to be successful.

Of course, there are a lot more aspects to take into account when you want to go global, but regardless, if your intentions are good (as I know they are), all these will be common sense to you. You see, for many women, having a business is a way of being able to make a living while spending more time at home. Although this can be great, it is not how you become global. It takes time to build a business, it takes time to sustain a business, and it takes even more time to push a business to the point of achieving an international position.

But in the end it's all worth it, believe me!

I've got a secret for you….come a little closer!

The Women's Edge Magazine (www.thewomensedgemag.com) is my "international" door and is currently distributed in 23 countries all over the world. Although it can seem overwhelming at first, in reality going global is not that difficult. One big challenge I see my clients having to face has nothing to do with the extent of their market share, but has everything to do with how comfortable they are with what they have to offer.

When you are not all upfront and proactive about your services, it usually means that you doubt their efficiency or validity. What a shame! How can you expect to sell something if you doubt it's any good yourself? Now, one thing I also see nearly every time is that the quality of the offer is rarely in question, it's just the value of the business owner herself. Let's face it: If you don't own what you offer to the point where it is hard for you not to scream about it out loud from the rooftops, then revisit your offer and work on your self-worth before anything else. This book offers great information to help you.

But I'd like to help you get on the right track first, so here are a few tips to get you started:

1. If you don't feel comfortable with your offer, if you can't talk about it without worrying about feedback, this means something is off. If you are unclear, your prospects will be even more so. Lack of clarity = fear = no purchase! In the global marketplace, this means a lack of credibility and you'll lose any chance of getting clients.

    Advice: Revisit your offer with the Love Radar. Make sure what you offer is based on what you really love to do and not what you think will sell. Remove any element that does not feel truly aligned with who you are. Then write your sales copy based on all the love elements you've gathered for the same offer. Love element = the transformation you offer your clients.

2. Align your pricing with the world market, not just within your country. I have another business in the French-speaking market and the price range is quite different. The way I price my offers is based on the time of interaction I have with clients, so of course programs will always be in a higher price range than products. However, in France for example, everything is expensive and the common belief is that if it is cheap, it's not good. You must take that public perception into consideration. Now, in the English-speaking market, the big players are the U.S., Canada, Australia, and the U.K. Apart from the U.K., all types of dollars are almost equal and way below the U.K. pricing range. However, I chose to use a $$$ pricing policy as it appeals to most people and seems more affordable to my U.K. clients. And yes, if there is a currency to choose when working globally, it is dollars, just because it is so well-known and also because in many countries it allows savings to be made due to the exchange rate.

   Advice: Do some market research, check out what other businesses' price ranges are in the country you'd like to enter, and align your prices! Don't expect that just because you come from X, Y, or Z land that you are better, because you are not. A rule of thumb is to align your prices, then raise them when appropriate.

3. The visual aspect of your business is really important. I know I've read some guru somewhere saying that "pretty doesn't sell." Well, let me tell you that my designs show off the level of quality my clients can expect. My offers are not in the lower price range, but everything is 5-star quality from A to Z, which includes all visuals.

   Advice: Make sure you hire the right graphic designer, who will be able to represent in image form what you are really about through colors, textures, shapes, and display. In the same way that a store needs to dress its window to invite customers to walk in, you must do the same in the huge shopping mall that is the online market. Don't forget that you have about 5 seconds to capture your potential client's attention. The right design will help you achieve just that. It will also make you look professional and will appeal to the global market.

4. Decide on 2 strategies you want to use to help you reach out globally. Do you want to focus on product development or on group programs? Do you want to be writing or speaking? You'll need to decide, then based on your strategy, identify ways that you can carry these strategies forward in your business.

    Advice: If you decide that speaking is going to be your strategy for 2013, then you'll need to make sure everything you do is aligned with it. Start with creating your media kit so it reflects what you have to offer to the audience. Structure your speech so it dovetails in with your offers. Don't speak about gardening if your business is all about cooking! You'd be surprised how many times I see that. Speaking can be a great tool to propel your business to the next level, but only if you do it right. Accepting all speaking opportunities without question is not the right way to go.

5. If you want opportunities to work with people in other countries, be willing to travel at your own expense. Today, unless you are already a big shot, most likely you'll need to prove your worth before anything else. It's an investment in yourself and in your business, so do it, but do it wisely.

So, let's do it—let's start today:

- Decide which part of the world you'd like to enter into.

- Research their culture and their way of conducting business online.

213

- Do they speak English? If not, is the niche you are aiming at most likely to speak English?

- Meet people from that country virtually at first through Facebook or LinkedIn.

- Find business organizations in the major cities and see if there is a group you'd love to attend (mix vacation with work).

- Identify the gap, what they don't have currently available to them, and fill it.

- Create your own workshop and travel, spreading your message as you go.

Conclusion

What you've witnessed through the pages that you just read is that there is no single way to build, run, and grow your business. However, what you need is courage, strength, dedication, resilience, creativity, and—most important of all—the ability to be yourself.

I hope you have enjoyed reading the wisdom of these amazing women just as much as I did. Go back to this book as often as you need to. And don't hesitate to contact them. All their contact information is provided. Don't be shy or ashamed. I can promise you that they'll be more than happy to answer all your questions.

In addition, what I enjoy most about my business is being able to collaborate with so many different women all over the world. And the best part? When I get to help them organize their very own collaborative work. That is where my real talent lies.

Without doubt, a book is THE 'Asset' to have to increase your visibility tenfold, to gain instant credibility and to increase your clientele. So, if you want to turn your dream of publishing your own anthology book into reality, get in touch with me and I'll show you how, together, we can accomplish this in 90 days, cost-free, going through everything from A to Z........ and how you can actually make money right from the very start.

Sounds good? Then email me at christine@coachingandsuccess.com.

Have a wonderful life running your successful business!

~Christine Marmoy

The End!

CPSIA information can be obtained at www.ICGtesting.com
Printed in the USA
BVOW011107160513

320906BV00005B/32/P